The PyramIT of Purpose

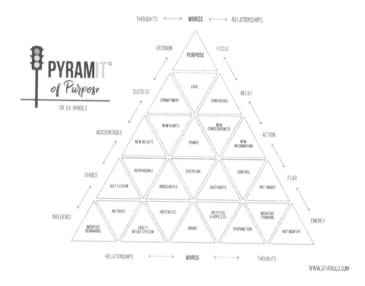

The ~~Secret~~ System to Living the Life You Truly Deserve

The PyramIT of Purpose

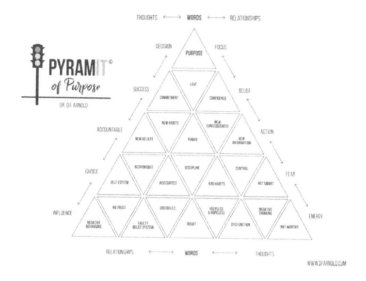

The ~~Secret~~ System to Living the Life You Truly Deserve

BY

Dr. D.F. Arnold

www.bookstandpublishing.com

Published by
Bookstand Publishing
Morgan Hill, CA 95037
4554_2

ISBN 978-1-63498-568-0

Printed in the United States of America

Dedication

This book is dedicated to everyone who reads it, and has the courage to discover their POWER to accomplish everything they have been PURPOSED to achieve. Your PURPOSE has been locked inside your mind waiting for you to discover it. When you apply the concepts in this book, your entire life will change. What was once viewed as an obstacle, will now be viewed as an opportunity for you to step into your PURPOSE.

Acknowledgements

I would like to give honor to everyone, everything and every situation that has given me the knowleged and wisdom to write this book. I now understand, that mistakes are only lessons to help teach us the way through this maze called "Life".

Table of Contents

Welcome to
<u>The PyramIT of Purpose</u>
<u>The Workbook</u>

Congratulations on your commitment to improve the quality of your personal and professional life! You are about to join thousands of others who have invested in and experienced the amazing benefits of this book. I am honored and excited you have allowed me to move through this journey with you.

This book was written to reiterate the main points of <u>The PyramIT of Purpose </u>and as you work through this book, please take the time to complete the notes sections. You will find them important in accelerating the process of creating change and moving upwards toward making a committed decision to change your Mood, Feelings, and Attitude (MFA), to ultimately discover your "IT."

The assignment sections will add to your success and will be a place to capture the key concepts and action items of each session. This simple

1

system will help you maximize the benefits of your experience.

I am a firm believer that we all have an "IT," that we should be living our purposes, and that our daily activities are worth recording. What is IT you may ask? IT is your purpose, and your purpose is to WIN, and when you WIN, the world wins. Therefore, in addition to the written exercises, take a few moments each day to jot down notes about the events in your life: how are you feeling, what are you are pleased with, what are you excited about, and acknowledge the positive changes you are making.

There is value in putting your thoughts, ideas, and feelings on paper and a level of clarity that comes with it. It is truly a simple, yet rewarding, process!

To get the most from your notes sections, here are a few things that may help:

1   Each day, Monday through Friday, listen to a CD and read an inspirational quote from Doc's Daily Dose.

2   After listening to the CD and choosing a quote of the day, open your journal and take immediate action on the days assignment.

3   Before you finish and close your book for the day, take a few minutes to reinforce what you have learned by jotting down any additional thoughts or feelings regarding what you learned and how you're going to use the progress you have made.

Now let's get to it! I know you must be ready to get started. There are wonderful and exciting things in store for you as you journey through this program. Have fun and until we meet in person, remember to...

Live "IT"!

Warmest regards,

Dr. D.F. Arnold

Dr. D.F. Arnold

Introduction

The thing that changes your life faster than anything else is making a decision that something in your life MUST change. We must decide and commit to breaking those habits that have caused us to continue to stay in the place where we've become so unhappy.

It's time to change the narrative you have become used to sharing with others. The narrative that allows you to feel sorry for yourself about the choices you've made in the past. Isn't it interesting how we know the people who will allow us to feel sorry for ourselves? These people won't give us the tough love we need because they need us to stay in our current position, because they feel sorry for themselves, and without us they will have to find someone else to share in their misery.

I'm not a guru, I'm only here to help you open the gifts inside you that have been lying dormant.

Dr. D.F. Arnold

Thoughts

We are where we are today because of the way we have processed the experiences in our life. Our lives to this point have been products of what our thoughts told us was possible. Our lives are a residual of what we think.

It is time to get back what you deserve; all the things you lost, all the things that are literally yours waiting to come back into your possession. Are you ready to fight, or are you going to keep giving the things that are rightfully yours, that God or the universe, whichever you subscribe to, said you could have from the beginning of time? Will you die and let the things you had the power to receive just sit in the warehouse with thousands of other undelivered packages addressed to people who gave up on their dreams just like you have been doing up until this point?

All of the experiences you have gone through were preparing you to take back the position that was designed for you. Does it really make sense that you have gone through hell to get to where you are, and you continue to allow the enemy to take what's yours? To steal your destiny? To have you convinced that you don't deserve to live a life of greatness? After all you've been through, does it make sense to keep losing the battle that starts in your mind, and ends in your actions, or inaction?

It's time to realize that the war or storm that's going on in your life is over your "PURPOSE", and the "IT" inside of you that can change not only your life, but the world. You have something in you that was designed for you, and because you have been allowing storms and distractions to detract you from being all you were called to be, these distractions are taking away what is YOURS. It is our unwillingness to see things the way they are, and not worse than they are, and our refusal to acknowledge the dysfunction we have been living in. It is time for us to learn from past failures and become more equipped with the tools needed in order to move to the next level.

We have allowed fear, doubt and the other words at the bottom of the PyramIT to alter the LIFE we deserve. We have allowed in-action to steal our dreams, and the unfortunate part is that we have allowed this to happen without a fight.

We have allowed the storms of life to take the purpose that was rightfully ours because we don't understand that IT is ours. When we see others with things we think are great, we just see them as being lucky instead of realizing that the majority had to work, and the most important part of the work they did was in their mind. The work that is done in OUR minds to change our thoughts to believing that we can indeed make that which once seemed impossible, to become possible, is merely a choice to change what we believe. When we begin to focus our energy on believing that we can, in spite of the obstacles or limits, we will start to move to the next level in our journey to discover our IT.

The negative behaviors and thoughts you have been dealing with didn't just happen. Those things were sent to stop you from becoming all you were supposed to be. We have accepted things in our lives and even adapted our way of living to negative circumstances, in turn creating an acceptance to them and viewing them as normal.

It's time to FIGHT. You're not too young or too old. David was 12 when he slayed Goliath, and Moses was up in age when he led his people to the promise land. We are never too young or old to fight for what belongs to us; we just have to make up our minds that we deserve it, our family deserves it, and the world deserves to experience the great things that we have inside of us. It doesn't matter how you fight and as a matter of fact, to fight for your future, it's going to be UGLY.

The fight for your stuff will be ugly, but it will be worth it. It's time to stop letting the enemy punk us out of what's ours. It's time to get angry, because generations have lost out on so much, and we continue to do what we've always done only receiving what we've always received. If you are ready to fight for what's yours, allow me to help you learn skills and tools to help you along the way. I wish to arm you with equipment that will help you fight through the storms and come out on the other side, possessing what is YOURS. I want to help you discover your IT.

You woke up today for a reason, and it's time to take over in this season. However, thanks to seasons, there is both sun and rain. Some of the situations you go through will be turbulent; it may seem as though you are in quick sand, sinking lower and lower into the depths of situations you have dreaded. You may have a yearning inside of you that something should change, but many times we don't understand what and how this change can take place.

You may be attempting to do the right thing, but the wrong thing continues to happen in and around your life. You may have had conversations with yourself about your desires to change, but you've never been able to figure out what and how to do it. We have negotiated with ourselves to change, we have made promises to ourselves and others to change, but these changes we so desperately seek continue to allude us.

We are truly in a battle for what we feel like we deserve. We are in a fight to accomplish goals, dreams, and ideas that have been placed in us since the beginning of our existence. There are miracles hidden deep inside of all of us; miracles to change not only our own lives but the lives of people all over the world.

The reason we struggle to access this deepest part of our being is because only a few people actually understand their hidden secrets enough to fully apprehend and access this POWER. This is the power that could change the world. But we are constantly under attack to stay "asleep" to this ability we all possess. With access to this POWER, our life changes in an instant, as do the lives of the people around us, because they can choose to follow in your steps and change as well.

The truth behind the hidden secret of this power is that you will be under a constant attack from a force that is far weaker than the power you have access to. But it's a force meant to discourage, distract, and disrupt you from accessing this power.

You have this power inside of you, and it is continuously trying to give you a glimpse of everything you possess. But until you break from the limiting beliefs that have been bestowed upon you from others who are reluctant to access this POWER, you will remain in a powerless position. You have always had access to this power, but unfortunately many times we have given this power away to our lesser self.

We all have the ability to expand our current situation, but we must realize that when we make the decision to do so, we will experience heavy opposition from the force wanting us to stay in the position we are currently in. This force will only fight us when we make a decision to do and be something different. If we stay exactly where we are and never attempt to move forward, then we won't experience this opposition.

Point 1: Our pain has a place in the position we strive to achieve. Many times we see pain as a bad thing instead of viewing pain as a point in our story that has the ability to make us strong enough to push toward the next part of our life. In many cases, pain is the conduit to launch us into our "PURPOSE". Pain can be a bad thing if we don't see it for what it really is, and we allow it to paralyze us in an attempt to keep us from going in the direction that the pain was really designed to have us go in. Pain has a point, and those words in the red, at the bottom of the PyramIT are experienced by all of us at some point. People often stay at the bottom without understanding that they have the ability to move up the PyramIT at any time. Once a person takes an honest look at where he/she is accepting pain and chooses to purposely move in a different direction, they take control of their future.

The unfortunate part of pain is that we allow it to keep us in a place of discontentment. It tricks us into thinking we aren't worthy of having more due to past experiences, what we were born into, and/or what our environment has or hasn't allowed. This pain can cause us to inflict pain on ourselves and on the people around us. We may feel hate toward ourselves. This sometimes causes us to hate the people around us for the situations we are in. This hate can cause us harm that doesn't show as a physical mark others can see, but many times this pain is so deeply rooted inside that we express it through dysfunctional actions like drugs, alcohol, rebellion or even suicide.

We allow this pain to attack what could be a prosperous future; a future that could've broken the cycle of discontentment, denial, and dysfunction running rampant in our family's history. The pain has caused us to react instead of think about what life could become. Pain doesn't always allow us time to figure things out, because we can become overwhelmed by it. Pain often causes us to stop believing. What we don't believe, we will never achieve. Pain can stop us from being who we were destined to be. The pain of regret, the pain of all of these words at the bottom of the PyramIT.

The pain is designed to stop you, but it can't if you become committed to discovering your purpose. When we are about to step into our purpose by making the decision to chase after IT, there will be a storm to try to stop you. The storm might not seem like it's connected to your success of finding your IT, but it is.

There is something in all of us that we are supposed to do and we are supposed to become—

our purpose, our IT. The storms in life are placed in our lives to stop us from achieving our IT. This force that works against you knows it can't stop you unless it robs you of your "FOCUS." This force that attempts to disrupt your destiny only has the power we give it. It can't stop us unless we allow it to. It has no power, except the power we give it. Learning lessons from the mistakes we make is paramount to passing the tests these storms create. When we go through something, it's important to learn the lessons of how to conquer those trials for next time, eventually helping us move to the next level. Unfortunately, many people get stuck at a certain level because they are unwilling to accept that something bad or unpleasant happened and see the reality of it by moving toward forgiving themselves and others to grow from the experience.

The storms and problems we experience are there to help us get stronger, to learn how to move up the PyramIT of purpose. These tough experiences have the power to distract us and kill our dreams. Bad experiences have killed the dreams of many people, mostly because they didn't understand that hidden deep within them they had the power to disrupt the unwanted circumstances they found themselves in. We have the power to agree or disagree with whichever situation we find ourselves in. How we choose to react to those storms is a major indicator of the success that we will have.

We have the ability to continuously create new realities, ones that allow us to dream about better circumstances regardless of what your current reality looks like. We have the ability to skip stages and place ourselves on the level that helps us look at the pain and the storm differently. For example, when a person passes away, it's painful. Then you look at the life they lived and you evaluate how that person lived prior to their death. Was it a life to the fullest, or did they die with music and a song left inside that was never played? If that was the case, how can you understand the importance of living life to the fullest, with the realization that unfortunately we all only get one life. Another example: Your company decided to downsize and you were let go. However, you always wanted to go back to school or start a business. What can you do to move forward with these goals instead of question why you got fired? We all have the power to accept the current reality, not see things as worse than they have to be, and make a decision to create what we would like our life to look like now. Storms and the pain they bring cause us to behave and do things that are unorthodox, and act beneath the level in which we are entitled to live.

When we make a decision that we deserve more, and we deserve a life we dream of, our life changes. The day we use our "ENERGY" to "FOCUS" on what can be, instead of what hasn't been, is the moment our life changes.

A storm hits in an attempt to distract you, but you can see it as hitting to prepare you for the directions that you are hoping to go in. Your mind is saying you should do this, but the other mind is telling you that you don't want to do it, that nothing will change, you're too old, no one has ever done it, and who are you to think that you can do it.

If everyone was to discover their IT and move toward achieving their IT, then the world would be changed. The book The Secret, wasn't about it being a secret, as much as it was about this "POWER" we have given in to that could've change our lives, our family's lives, and lives of others around the world. If this negative power continues to keep you at the bottom of the PyramIT and you never believe or choose to climb any higher than the people around you, then you won't see that it's possible to get it done.

Unfortunately, many will never attempt to change from the situations that have kept them at the bottom.

It's not about you, it's about what you can do to change the world. It is about your influence and what you are trying to get done. Think about the times when things happened in your life, things you couldn't control, you must now see how they have been distractions to waste the limited time you had to get something done that could've changed your life and allowed you to enjoy the reason you were born. The storm, issues, and problems we face are distractions to keep us from being all that we were destined to become.

You're fighting against a force that knows how powerful you can be if you utilize the "POWER" inside of you. That's why the enemy fights to keep you unaware and lazy to this power you possess by providing distractions meant to prevent you from finding your IT. You are a threat if you discover your IT. We must endure through these storms in order to perform the miracles in our lives and in the lives of others. When we begin to break down these walls and barriers to move up the PyramIT to get to our "PURPOSE", everything changes. When you wake up to rebuke the storms in your life and demand the best out of yourself.

The storm can't stop you from pursuing your IT when you are determined to have IT, so it will try to make deals with you along the way by offering you less than you are worth. Your "CONCIOUSNESS" may be happy with it, because it was more than you had before, but in reality, it is still less than you deserve. This is the trick of a storm: it loves attacking you, it loves when you give up and give in to it, it loves hearing you say what you can't do or what you can't become. Storms have done this to millions of people, but there are some who have realized their IT and pursued their true calling regardless of where on the PyramIT they started. Those people understood that the things the storm convinced them they couldn't obtain were self-inflicted. The storm tricked them into doing these "DYSFUNCTIONAL" things to themselves. We didn't do these things to ourselves; this way of thinking was passed down by others and became our reality because we believed they knew what they were talking about. Our environment is a big contributor to us believing what we can and can't become and even our loved ones have influenced our thoughts of unworthiness, negative thinking, doubt, hopelessness, and helplessness.

The storm convinces us that we were nothing, and we were never going to become anything great because we came from nothing. In reality we came from the most powerful seed in the universe. It convinces us we will never get out of the situations or states we're in, we can never be loved because of all of our insecurities and mistakes, we can never be blessed, and we will never be free from the bad habits we have formed.

Some aren't just dealing with one enemy. What you're fighting against is a strategic force working to get you away from that which is in you to change your family background, community and the world. These enemies are organized to pull you away from the power inside you that can do great things. This power is coming to bring you down, kill your dreams, and take what you have that can change the world. The reason why you are so young going through what you're going through and the reason some of you have been dealing with dysfunction, fear and no trust since you were young, is because the enemy knew years ago how much power you had to change the world if you understood the power within you. The negative force distracts you by allowing the storms, but gives you small victories. It keeps your power on a leash, only allowing you to go so far and gain access to only a few doors to keep you passively thinking this is good enough, or I'm doing better than them so I guess I'm doing ok.

It's when you begin to create a new belief of what's possible and develop new strategies and habits that replace the old behaviors that you move to a new level on consciousness. It's not about where you are now, but where you can go, your destiny to discover your IT. It is about the people you will influence and that will influence you. Those people who will connect with your spirit.

The people who will influence you to, discover your IT, go to school, finish your degree, learn and believe in what's possible. Helping you to Focus on knowing that nothing is IMPOSSIBLE FOR THOSE who believe.

You can't allow your fear and doubt to have more power over your faith to believe what is possible for your life. You have to believe that you have more power than your fear and doubt, and the only power it has is the power you give it.

It's time for us to stand up and become who we were destined to become. We will never be what we were destined to be if we hang out at the bottom of the PyramIT. We can never reach our IT from there.

You can't be what you were destined to be when you hang out with people whose constant conversation is about limits and obstacles, people who are constantly critical about discovering new information. It's time to come out of your cave of old ways of thinking and believing. Tell yourself that even with your insecurities, you're going to utilize the energy within you to develop relationships with others who have different thought processes than yours.

You must commit to discovering IT by not allowing people, situations, or procrastination to hold you back. You must trust that by breaking bad habits, discovering new information, and developing new relationships your life will change. You must believe you can overcome the storms. Your energy and movement during the storms can propel you toward your IT. When you discover you have everything you need to attack this storm to win is the day you have learned how to have victory.

The problem isn't if we have something, we definitely have something special inside of us, the problem is we don't know what we have.

Mark Twain said, "Inherently, each one of us has the substance within to achieve whatever goals or dreams we define. What is missing from each of us is the training, education, knowledge, and insight to utilize what we already have." Imagination is the key ingredient to our thoughts. Imagination can take us anywhere.

I once heard a story about a very wealthy gentleman who didn't have many friends, and for years he lived in his big mansion with no one but his servants whom he barely spoke to. His servants knew not to initiate conversation with this man because they heard from past employees that this could result in termination. As years went by, the wealthy man became lonely and started researching animals that could carry on a conversation and not require too much from its master. After learning about a parakeet that lived in the African jungles, the man decided to take a trip to get one.

Upon arriving in the jungle, he was astonished by all of the parakeets and how they were carrying on conversations just like humans. He saw the one he wanted, captured it, and took it home. The gentleman was so wealthy he gave the parakeet nothing but the finest food, water, and his cage was shaped like the mansion it resided in. The man treated this parakeet very well and as the years went by, the wealthy gentleman bonded deeply with his pet. As he was about to travel near where he had captured his friend, he asked the bird if it had a message he would like him to tell the village about how he was doing. The bird thought for a moment and said "Yes. Please tell my friends that I'm eating quite well and I'm happy in my huge cage." The man said "Okay" and headed out the next day.

After conducting his business, he headed to the village and went to the jungle where he had captured the parakeet years before. When he arrived, he told the other animals to gather around as he had a message from their friend. As all of the animals gathered around, he shared with them the message his parakeet had sent. "He told me to tell you that he's eating well and he's happy in his huge cage." When he finished, he saw one of the parakeets in a tree nearby making a loud noise and as he looked at him, he saw what could only be described as the bird crying. After a couple of seconds, the bird fell from the tree and died. The man thought the bird must have really loved and missed his friend.

When he arrived back home, his parakeet was very happy to see him, and as the man settled next to his bird's cage he began to tell it about his trip. The parakeet asked about his village and what happened. The wealthy gentleman began to describe how all of the birds gathered around to hear the message. The man told his parakeet that one bird in particular must have really loved him, because he started crying and fell off his tree and died. As he finished telling the story to his parakeet, it made the same sound as the bird in the village and when the man looked at his parakeet, its eyes were watery and it fell in its cage and died. The wealthy gentleman was very distraught and after a while, he removed the bird from its cage, took it outside and laid it on the ground. He began to dig a hole to bury it when the bird flew to the nearest tree.

"Why did you do that? Why did you trick me?" the wealthy gentleman asked.

"Because of the message I received from my friend," the bird said.

"What was the message that made you trick me?"

"The message was simple. He said in order for me to be free and live, I must die to what I have been imprisoned to."

That's what we need to do in order to live our purpose and discover our IT. We need to die to what has imprisoned us for too long. The biggest thing we have been imprisoned by is a faulty belief system, and in order for us to grow, we must escape from the old ways of thinking, and live new ways of thinking that require us to be at a whole different level of consciousness.

The concept in this book is designed to help you realize how this faulty way of thinking has been passed down from generation to generation, but it's time for you to break the cycle and live the life you've truly desired.

The most valuable commodity we possess is our imagination.

We have the ability to pull almost anything we can visualize toward ourselves. This means that anything we really focus on can be attracted to us like a magnet. The Law of Attraction exists and it has been practiced for thousands of years. For those that really believe it, their lives have changed. This Law is indestructible and can't be destroyed. However it can be hidden in plain sight from those who are unwilling to release their current way of viewing their circumstances. The answer is always right in front of you using this law of attraction, yet we turn away from it and to other things to figure out the solution to our problem.

Growing up in our environments we are taught to believe in those things we can understand. If we can't understand it, then we believe there is no way it can work. It must be logical in order for our brain to process and verify its validity.

To comprehend our purpose or our IT, we have to believe and understand: (1) what lies deep in all of us this eminent power (our IT), and (2) this power is impartial and unemotional. We all have this power, this IT, and creating our own success happens when we identify with our IT, understand what it is, and how to use it correctly.

The first step is to acknowledge you are worthy of all the success you will find. You must continue to understand during this process that you are worthy, you deserve your IT, and you will discover IT. We all need to be somewhat reprogrammed.

The discovery of your IT will be easy. The hard part will be breaking down the barriers that attempt to stop you from becoming your better, stronger self.

Even though there is so much going on in the world, you must see the world as beautiful, because you're responsible for how you respond to what happens in the world. If God, the universe, or whatever you subscribe to, wanted to change the world, do you really think it would be a problem for it to happen? Absolutely not, which means that everything has happened or that is happening is because it is supposed to. You only need to respond knowing that what happens is up to you.

When you become "PURPOSEFUL" with your thoughts, you understand it is all a process meant to separate the people who really want it and are willing to grow and learn the system, from those who want to continue getting the results from remaining in their dysfunction.

When you commit to the journey to discover your purpose, you will discover things changing around you. You will notice people asking you questions because they notice the change in you. Maybe you're not hanging out anymore, or maybe you are reading more, whatever it is, they will notice the new conversation that comes from you. Take those opportunities to teach what you've learned. You may not have it all together, but you know deep down you have found your IT.

The world has changed for the better. If you look back through history, we never could have imagined America having a Black President, or that so many people of color would live affluent lives. However, we still have a lot of work to do, which is one of the main reasons I encourage everyone to discover their IT. I imagine a world where everyone recognizes they have something special inside that can change the world.

The evolution that will take place when people understand their IT and use it, will shift inner city communities, rural environments, and places all over the world.

The process for you to change will be simple. What will be difficult is you deciding enough is enough and it's time for you to change. It's the same thing with money. I once heard motivational speaker Les Brown say that it wasn't hard for him to make a million dollars, the hard part was believing that he could do it.

We must not complicate the process. We must relax, believe, and watch it happen. Everything is perfect and everything will flow to you.

We must use our imagination to stimulate our feelings into believing we have that which we say we want before everyone else sees it. We must remember our mind doesn't know the difference between fact and fantasy.

Some people have trouble visualizing or imagining what their life could be like due to only focusing on the reality of the way things currently look in their life. We must develop our imagination to create the life we deserve, because this ability allows us to change our world. We can develop this by looking at magazines that possess those things we have dreamt about, taking a trip to a fancy neighborhood, or allowing ourselves a couple minutes a day to let go and fantasize about what it would be like to live the life we want.

If you can create an image of yourself living your IT life, knowing all the things you could offer the world, you will come alive. You will begin to awaken that IT inside of you to become that person.

You now have the tools to create in your imagination the way you want to see your life. You have accepted who you are and what you have done in the past. You project great energy. "Energy" that is full of confidence about being great in what you were purposed to do.

The only time people and their dysfunction can affect you is when you allow it. When you feel confident about your purpose and you are focused, disciplined, and committed to it, you realize that other people's problems are only distractions. You're not perfect and you don't need to be. You only need to stay persistent when it comes to your IT. You are getting stronger every day and you no longer put yourself in situations that cause you to revert back. This may be hard at first, but with time it will become easier and easier, because you are enjoying the person who you are becoming. Soon the weakness will continue to fall away.

You can use visualization to set your goals. All goals and the success that came from completing those goals came from a thought. Again, the reason why we must be specific is because once we begin creating what it is we have thought up, others will help us. If we aren't specific with our details they won't be able to understand what it is we need from them and this will cause confusion. In order to manifest our purpose, we can't be confused, we must be specific.

You must take time to look at your feelings and you must begin to make negative things less important. When you develop the technique of not stressing over things that attempt to pull your focus away from your purpose, you begin to move toward your IT. To live in abundance is to understand that the world is abundant. To operate in purpose is to understand, contrary to what your tribe (family) taught you, that you deserve IT. To have the experiences you imagine, will require you to have money and resources. To obtain these things will require you to have a thought process different than what you once had. The world has taught you there is a scarcity and there isn't. There is an abundance of anything and everything we need.

When you begin to see yourself as more prosperous, you will be able to buy the experience. Your visualization creates a movie in which you are the director and you become responsible for hiring and firing any idea that does not line up with the plot you have created to reach your IT. You are in control of every scene in your life. You are determined to create the lifestyle of your choosing. If you don't have what you need, you will create it. Most people miss the simplicity of this because they don't understand the PyramIT of Purpose and the "POWER" they have to create the life they deserve.

Day 1 — The Decision

Your life changes when you make the decision to not repeat the choices you made in the past.

Successful Life Formula:

1. Expect your outcome to be great.

2. Decide to take action.

3. Notice what is happening in your life due to your current actions.

4. If you are not receiving the results you would like, change your approach.

One way to save time in reaching your goals is by using role models or mentors to accelerate your success.

1. Look for people who are already achieving the success you want.

2. Speak with them about what they are doing.

3. Emulate what they do.

It is impossible to fail if you learn the lessons from your mistakes!

YOUR ASSIGNMENT:

1. Write two decisions you have been putting off that, when you make them, will change your life dramatically.

   _____

   _____

   _____

   _____

   _____

   _____

2. Now that you have made a committed decision, take action immediately. To do this, write down the first few steps:

   - What are four simple things you could do right now that would be consistent with your new decisions? For example, if you decided to eat healthier, what can you do with the junk food in your house right now?

   - Who could you call to talk about your decisions?

   - To what could you commit?

   - What letter could you write?

- When you're tempted, what could you do instead of giving in to your old behavior?

_____

_____

_____

_____

_____

_____

_____

_____

Remember: *"The point of power is in the present!"*

"ACTION" is the key. Never think of something you would like to have or do without taking action toward that goal. This will create a snowball effect, thus momentum toward achieving your goals.

Dr. D.F. Arnold

Day 2 — Understanding the Role

Ultimately, everything we do in our lives is driven by our fundamental need to avoid getting hurt and our need to receive things enjoyable. The choices we make in our lives are driven by the need to receive enjoyment, and this enjoyment constitutes a controlling force in our lives. We will do far more to avoid being hurt than we will to have enjoyment. Hurt is a better motivator in the short term.

Whatever your Mood, Feelings, and Attitudes (MFA's) are at any moment is what is most real to you. Therefore, if you want to change your behaviors, you must change your mood, feelings, and attitudes. Once you begin noticing and changing those three things, you will be able to change your focus and attention on:

1. How not changing your current behaviors is more hurtful than changing.

2. How changing will bring you enjoyment and allow you to have the life you deserve.

You cannot control the thoughts that present themselves in your head, but you can control the ones you meditate or focus on. You must associate new thoughts with the things that have hurt you in the past in order to change your behavior. To take complete control of your life, you must make a decision to change the choices you have made in the past. The power is in the decision and the motivation is in the action.

Use the hurtful things that have happened to you, instead of being used by what has hurt you!

YOUR ASSIGNMENT:

Explore the following statements.

1. Three new actions I know I should take now:

_____

_____

_____

_____

_____

_____

2. The hurt I have associated with these actions that has kept me from following through:

_____

_____

_____
_____
_____
_____

3. What enjoyment did I receive from <u>not</u> following through on these three actions?

_____
_____
_____
_____
_____
_____

4. For each of these actions, describe what you have to lose if you don't follow through.

_____
_____
_____
_____
_____
_____

5. What have I, or will I, miss out on? What can be taken away from me?

_____
_____

_____

_____

_____

_____

6. What are the benefits I will gain by taking action in each of these areas now? How will it make my life better? How will it create joy, happiness, success, and freedom?

_____

_____

_____

_____

_____

_____

Day 3 — Choices

What controls our lives are our choices, and the choices we have made to this point have caused us to experience hurt or enjoyment. It is our hurtful experience or enjoyment that has contributed to our Mood, Feelings and Attitudes (MFA). These three things determine our behaviors. Therefore, if we want to change our behavior we must make a decision to change our choices.

If we want to change our lives, we must focus on the things we can control. You cannot control everything that happens in your life, but you can control the way you respond to those events and what thoughts you link to the events that have taken place.

1. When you begin to link positive associations with the negative things that have happened in your life, you begin to take control. This allows you to take the power away from any situation that continues to add pain and discourse to your life and control it yourself.

2. We must reinforce positive outcomes from those negative things that have taken place. We must take control of our MFAs in order to take control of our life.

   The action of associating different thoughts with those old thoughts will bring about new behaviors.

Always continue to ask yourself, "What are the negative associations I've made in the past that have kept me from taking the action steps needed to achieve the life I deserve?"

Your MFAs control your level of motivation. Every action step you take has an effect on your future.

1. Everything we think or do causes things to happen.

2. Our MFAs are going to have an effect on our lives.

3. The results of these thoughts build on each other and take our lives in a particular direction.

For every direction, there is an ultimate place where you end up. This place always affects our MFAs. It is important to ask ourselves: What would I like my life and my future to look like? What do I want my life to be about?

While we may not know precisely how our future will look, we can determine the kind of person we want to be. We can make the decision of how we will live our lives going forward based on the idea of becoming that person.

Thinking about the bigger picture will pull us through some of the short-term tough times and allow us to keep things in perspective. This will allow us to remain happy, fulfilled, and driven to focus our MFAs on our dreams.

YOUR ASSIGNMENT:

1. Two things I have done in the past that have shaped my future positively:

_____

_____

_____

_____

_____

_____

2. Two things that I have done in the past that have been disempowering:

_____

_____

_____

_____

_____

_____

3. Write down the decision you will make that will change these negative associations today.

_____

_____

_____

_____

_____

_____

*When we become aware of these
disempowering beliefs that zap our power,
we break the pattern of allowing our
unconscious conditioning to control us.*

Day 4 — Your MFAs

To change an area in your Life you must change your MFAs and how you associate negative experiences with them. Three things must be in place for you to make these changes and to count on them to last. They are the six fundamentals of your MFAs:

1. Develop control of yourself. To do this, three levels of responsibility must take place and you must decide the following:

   a. Something must change.

   b. I must change it.

   c. I can change it.

2. Interrupt what you currently associate negative experiences with in your life. You must leave behind your former ways of thinking and feeling.

3. Condition a new, empowering association with your old ways of thinking.

4. Install a new way of thinking about your old experiences, and reinforce them until it becomes a habit. Any thought or behavior that is reinforced repeatedly will become a habit.

5. Link enjoyment to your new choices.

6. Reward yourself for small victories, and you will develop new patterns quickly.

YOUR ASSIGNMENT

Review the actions you listed yesterday, do the following:

1. Develop control. Five reasons why I must change that behavior now and why I know I can do it.

_____

_____

_____

_____

_____

_____

2. I must condition myself by practicing my new behavior. What will I do repeatedly until it becomes a habit and easier to do?

The PyramIT of Purpose

_____
_____
_____
_____
_____
_____
_____

Here is an effective, albeit outrageous, way to get leverage and break your bad behavior:

1. Get a study buddy and promise him/her and a group of other friends that you will begin to study or read a chapter from your book at least once a day. Further, commit that if you break your promise, you will eat a whole can of dog food.

The woman who shared this suggestion with me told me she and her friend kept their dog food cans in plain view at all times to remind them of their commitments. When they didn't feel like reading their book, they would pick up the can and read the label. Unappetizing ingredients like horsemeat chunks helped them achieve their goals without a hitch!

People want to change the way they react and feel about any situation that has negatively affected their life. They want to move from feeling discouraged to encouraged, from sad to happy, from emotionally weak to emotionally strong. Or they want to change their current behavior. For example, they want to stop overeating, they want to move from not studying and ultimately failing, to studying and receiving better grades; they want to move from taking no action, to taking action when it comes to exercising and enjoy it; they want to go from procrastination to following up on their commitments. The reason we want to change these behaviors is because we want to feel better about ourselves.

Everything we do is an attempt to change the way we feel ... to change our MFA.

What we do is powerfully shaped by our MFAs. When we are frustrated, we tend to behave differently than when we are feeling confident or excited. One of the most important things we can do to create the power, happiness, and the passion we really want in our lives is to learn to manage our MFAs. Your MFAs determine your behavior and your reactions. If you want to change your reactions to anything, the first thing you need to focus on is changing your MFAs.

You are always responsible for your MFAs. After the next few days of learning, you won't just be responsible, you will know how to quickly and easily change how you feel about virtually anything and move into a better place. You do this by learning how to control and direct the focus of your mind.

Your MFAs come from what you are focusing your attention on during any given moment. At any moment, you are erasing most of what is going on around you. That is: to feel bad, hurt, or in any way that has caused you pain, you have to erase (not focus on, not think about) everything that's good in your life. And vice versa. In order for you to feel good, energized, and happy, you have to erase the things that cause you to feel upset, mad, and hurt. This process of erasing is an important part of how the mind maintains the balance in one's emotional state. However, if this isn't in control, it will wreak havoc in your day-to-day experience.

To manage your MFAs, you can control two things with respect to focus. When you change either of these, you immediately change how you feel:

1. What you are thinking in your mind.

2. How you are thinking about it (i.e., receiving joy or happiness).

At this moment, how you are assessing things determines where you focus. Assessments are nothing but questions you ask yourself. Your MFAs and ultimately your life are the result of the questions you ask yourself. To manage your MFAs and gain control over what you focus on, you must control the questions you ask yourself. Try not to ask limiting, open ended questions. Begin asking yourself questions that empower you.

YOUR ASSIGNMENT:

1. Four questions I am going to ask myself every morning for the rest of this program. These are questions that will cause my MFAs to feel empowered:

   _____

   _____

   _____

   _____

   _____

   _____

2. Keep them with you at all times. Put sticky notes on your mirror, keep a copy in your wallet or purse, and have one on your nightstand.

3. Every morning ask yourself these four questions and come up with at least two answers.

Dr. Arnold's Morning Power Questions:

1. What makes me happy in my life right now? What about it makes me happy? How does that make me feel?

_____

_____

_____

_____

_____

_____

2. What excites me in my life right now? What about it makes me excited? How does that make me feel?

_____

_____

_____

_____

_____

_____

3. What makes me proud in my life right now? What about it makes me proud? How does that make me feel?

_____

_____

_____

_____

_____

_____

4. What makes me grateful in my life right now? What about it makes me grateful? How does that make me feel?

_____

_____

_____

_____

_____

_____

5. What things do I enjoy most in my life right now? What about it do I enjoy? How does that make me feel?

_____

_____

_____

_____

_____

_____

6. What commitment do I have in my life now? What about it makes me committed? How does that make me feel?

_____

_____

_____

_____

_____

_____

7. Who am I in love with? Who shows me love? What about it makes me feel loved? How does being loved make me feel?

_____

_____

_____

_____

_____

_____

Dr. D.F. Arnold

Days 5-6 — Values

Our values affect our MFAs, and our MFAs are based on the experiences that have happened to us in life. The things we value affect our MFAs, and this emotional state is based on the experiences we have had in our lives, and what we believe to be most important for us to experience (move closer to) or reject (move far away from).

The "moving closer to" values or "enjoyment" values, are emotions such as affection, joy, success, and safety. These are known as "ends values." It is important to define the difference between "means values" which are things, instruments, or byproducts, and "ends values" which drive our reasons for doing things and ultimately shape our behaviors as human beings. Some people may say that what they value most in life is their huge TV or their things. While it's true they may value a TV because it's important to them, they value it as a "means," a way to get what they are really after. The "ends" person who values a TV might be seeking a sense of accomplishment, status or depending upon the type of TV, a sense of fun.

Likewise, many people say they want to be rich. However, being rich is merely a means to an end. As Tony Robbins would say, "They don't want pieces of paper with pictures of 'deceased notables' on them. They want what they think being rich will give them." For some people, they believe being rich is a sense of security, the ability to be in control of their lives, having freedom, or a feeling of choice. The secret is to know what it is that you really want—the "end values."

Successful people understand the decisions they make are nothing but values clarification. When a person makes decisions based on what he/she values most and what they truly want most in life, they will find they can make decisions more effectively and rapidly. That is why successful people make a decision and move forward with it because they are always aware of what they value. If that value is only money, they make their decisions based on money.

A belief is a feeling of certainty about what something means.

Your beliefs will help you determine whether or not you feel like you are meeting your values and they will either limit or liberate you. That is why Henry Ford said, "If you think you can, or think you can't, you're right." You set up rules you live by based on your beliefs, even though some of the rules may be false, you still govern yourself by them. These rules become conditioned ideas that say, "If this is, then that happens."

Values are also very important because what we value will guide all the decisions we make. That's why we have to be real about what in the world is most important to us. We have to be absolutely clear.

YOUR ASSIGNMENT:

1. In my life right now, what is most important to me?

_____

_____

_____

_____

_____

_____

2. Write down how you would like to feel, the MFAs you most value, such as joy, passion, or

love, as opposed to means values like to be rich or successful. If you think you want to be rich or successful, ask yourself, "If I were rich, if I'm successful, what would I ultimately receive from it? How would it make me feel?" Those feelings are what guide your life, moving you closer to your values.

_____

_____

_____

_____

_____

_____

Examples of a Value:

1. Purpose (It)
2. Success
3. Love
4. Passion
5. Attitude
6. Discipline
7. Commitment
8. Confidence
9. Relationships
10. Energy
11. Thoughts
12. Happiness

13. Health
14. Intelligence
15. Growth
16. Contribution
17. Affection
18. Humor

3. My moving closer to values in the order of importance are:

_____

_____

_____

_____

_____

_____

Examples of a Hierarchy of Values:

1. New Beliefs
2. New Habits
3. New Level Of Conciousness
4. New Information
5. Health
6. Success
7. Happiness
8. Growth
9. Love
10. Contribution
11. Humor

12. Intelligence
13. Power

4. The MFAs I would do almost anything to avoid.

For some people, this list might include rejection, frustration, or loneliness. Discovering what you want to avoid will help you understand more about what drives you. We are not driven just to get the things we want. We are also driven to avoid those feelings we link negative feelings to, our moving away from values.

_____
_____
_____
_____
_____
_____

Examples of Values:

1. Negative Behaviors
2. Helplessness/Hopelessness
3. Faulty Belief System
4. Doubt
5. Dysfunction
6. Not Worthy
7. Relationships/Mood

8. Energy/Feelings
9. Thoughts/Attitude

5. My moving away from values in the order of their importance, starting with the one I would do the most to avoid feeling.

_____

_____

_____

_____

_____

_____

Examples of a Hierarchy of Values:

1. Negative Thinking
2. Bad Habits
3. Insecurities
4. Obstacles
5. No Trust
6. Anger
7. Frustration
8. Boredom
9. Resentment
10. Jealousy
11. Depression
12. Overwhelm
13. Self-Pity
14. Sadness

15. Worry

6. What has to happen in order for my MFAs to be in alignment?

For example, if success is one of your values, what has to happen for you to feel successful? On your moving away from values, what has to happen? For some individuals, if they lose a game, they feel like a failure. For others, they view failure as a learning experience, one they learn from, move on, and make it different the next time.)

_____

_____

_____

_____

_____

_____

Examples of MFAs for Moving Toward and Moving Away From Values:

1. "I feel healthy when I walk at least 15 minutes a day."

2. "I feel healthy when I take care of myself by getting massages."

3. "Whenever I eat fruit, I feel healthy."

4. "I would feel boredom if, and only if, all the world's problems have been solved."

5. "I would feel boredom if I cut off all contact with humanity and set up residence in Antarctica."

6. The things I am willing to change now to improve my life.

_____

_____

_____

_____

_____

_____

Examples of MFAs That Should Be Changed:

1. "If I made a mistake, I can't be successful."

2. "Because I didn't go to college, I'm not smart."

3. "If my children get into trouble, that means I'm a bad parent."

4. "Everyone in my family had cancer, so I will probably get it, too."

5. "To be a success, I have to be rich."

6. "Nobody in my family went to college, so there is no way I can go."

Day 7 — Beliefs

To gain the control you desire in your life, you must discover your core beliefs, change the ones that limit you from having the life you desire, and resolve any beliefs that are in conflict with one another. In order to change a belief, the following must take place:

1. Identify the belief or beliefs that you want to change.

2. Link negativity to your current belief so you choose to move away.

3. Identify a new belief that empowers you.

4. Link great enjoyment to the new belief.

5. Condition the new belief by practicing it— mentally imagining and feeling the effect of how your life will be changed for the better with this new belief, and how much it will continue to hurt if you keep the old belief.

There are two core beliefs I encourage you to adopt:

1. Today, not my past, affects my future.

2. If I am truly committed, a way will always lend itself to me.

Find three core beliefs that have limited your life up until this point.

1. Identify three beliefs you want to change.

2. Close your eyes. Think about the consequences you have experienced because of these limiting beliefs. Feel the emotional price these beliefs have had on your life. What price have you paid in your relationships, finances, physical body, and level of happiness? What do you regret and/or dislike most as a result of these beliefs?

3. Five years into the future, what is the price you are willing to pay for still having these limiting beliefs?

4. Ten years into the future, what is the price?

5. Twenty years into the future, what is the price, has the price changed?

6. Decide what you would like your new beliefs to be and write them down. Close your eyes and imagine how these beliefs will transform

the quality of your life. What will you gain by having these new beliefs? How will your life be more enjoyable? How will you be more successful in your finances and in your relationships? When these beliefs begin to guide your daily actions, how will your physical body be transformed? Associate how doing these things are making your life more fulfilling.

7. Five years in the future with your new beliefs, what does your life look like?

8. Ten years, what does your life look like?

9. Twenty years, what does your life look like?

10. Look at your life in the future and decide which of the two belief systems makes more sense to adopt, and then return to the present.

YOUR ASSIGNMENT:

1. Write down your old beliefs and what the consequences have been or would have been all your life in order to remind yourself of the leverage that will guide you in maintaining your new beliefs.

_____

_____

_____

_____

_____

_____

2. My two new beliefs are:

_____

_____

_____

_____

_____

_____

3. My new beliefs will increase the quality of my life by:

_____

_____

_____

_____

_____

_____

Energy

Energy is power and in order to create a new life, you must chose to give your energy to the things that have power to create change. This power begins with our words. When you begin to focus your mind on what is possible, you begin to understand that you are never a victim over any circumstance, you are a victor. There is nothing random about your life. It all has to do with how you perceive and react to every situation—the good and the bad—and your purpose can be achieved based on what you believe.

Everything that happened in your life came with a lesson. What if I never got kicked out of two different high schools? Would I have understood that failure is based on my actions or inactions? What if I was never kicked off my football team during my freshman year of high school? Would I have understood that football was an opportunity that I could use to go to college? What if I never went to speak with Dr. Scott, the person who conditionally allowed me in graduate school, because I had a conversation with him about wanting to change my community? Would I be the Dr. Damon Arnold I am today? All of these lessons worked together for the better. That didn't mean all of the things that happened to me were good at the time, but they worked together for the best.

Our life is like a puzzle from the time we are born until the time we die. All types of pieces make up this puzzle. Some of the pieces we chose, some of the pieces we didn't. Some of the pieces we put in, and other pieces were put in by other people. But when the puzzle is done, it creates a perfect picture that's full of a life. That life deserves to be lived to the fullest. We design this puzzle regardless of the pieces we have been given.

The puzzle is controlled by our choices. Our choices to finally say it's time for us to expect more. It starts with the thoughts that we believe can be true.

Life isn't always fair, but we can still win as long as we don't give up and continue to believe that we have the power to change any circumstance we are born into. This doesn't always happen, though, until we have made up our minds that it will be worth it, and it's necessary for us to achieve our purpose and finally break the cycle.

The attack of our minds or our thoughts means we have become a valuable asset to the world. When we have thoughts that can change our life, we will be hit with all kind of negative things. We are confronted with these negative situations and thoughts because if we begin to realize the power of possibility, we can move into a different level of consciousness that will literally change everything around us. These attacks are to discourage us into believing it's not possible due to bad experiences in the past. The attacks want to keep us locked at the lowest level of our awareness. These levels are often full of doubt, fear, and negative behaviors. The people around us will exhibit these same behaviors, which will cause our consciousness to believe this has to be right because everyone around us thinks these same disempowering thoughts.

Working on your mind is essential because what you think about, you bring about. You must focus on what you want to accomplish. Success leaves clues and you must find the people who are achieving this success and follow what they do.

It's best to monitor your relationships, as there are nurturing relationships and toxic relationships. Which ones do you allow to affect your life? The nurturing relationships will bring out the best in you, while the toxic relationships will drain you, and convince you that staying where you are is better than discovering who you were meant to be.

You can't overcome weakness by fighting it. You overcome weakness by leaving it behind. You do this by becoming aware of the things that keep you down, the things that keep you functioning in the old belief patterns. When you move yourself away from old behaviors, doubt, and dysfunction you used to hang on to, you are moving into a new realm of self-discipline and power. When you decide to operate in this power, even though it may be a battle initially, your mind will have to overcome the old, faulty information you used to believe. Your mind won't initially see the logic in attempting these new behaviors because it was accustomed to doing things the old way, to the point where your old beliefs were habits. However, in order to move up the PyramIT, you must make a choice to change your beliefs and move from the impossible to the possible. Your ability to move up the PyramIT and discover your IT will be predicated by how quickly you can turn what was once viewed by your consciousness as impossible to what is possible.

The PyramIT of Purpose

You must look at beliefs differently, because different things have been established telling us what isn't possible. These aren't laws, these are only made up beliefs we have created in our mind to stop us from attempting to do the great things we were destined to do. When turning beliefs into laws, we give our mind permission to stop attempting to try to break through. We see people breaking through these faulty beliefs and ways of thinking all the time, but yet we think it is only reserved for the lucky.

Recognize that you may be fighting generations of set ways of thinking and beliefs instilled in you since your inception. In order to become all you were meant to be, you have to make a decision to leave where you are right now. As you move away from your old energy, there will be a sense of loss because you are losing part of who you used to be in order to become who you were destined to be. Your main challenge will be to leave a version of your old self behind to become a newer version of yourself based on becoming the person you desire to be. This is your IT. As you move toward this new energy, you will find others who are moving up there PyramIT to discover their purpose, too.

Your imagination will help you through this sense of loneliness by allowing you to create and visualize the person you are moving toward. It will help you find joy in the new life you are creating for yourself. Everything around us is energy, from the places we inhabit, to our bodies, to the things we look at and the things we desire. Think of your energy as a warehouse that only houses things that have been ordered and whatever is ordered is then shipped out. If you want to live your IT, you must believe that it's possible and that you deserve it. You must start tricking your mind into believing that it's already happening.

You start by creating a vision board of what you want your life to look like. This includes your house, cars, job, and family life. Cut out the pictures and hang this board somewhere where you look at it several times a day.

Next, start going in the stores you will one day be shopping in. You can try on those expensive shoes and clothes you will one day be buying. When doing this, don't for even a second think that you're wasting the sales person's time. Change this way of thinking by focusing on the commission they will earn when you come back to the store to purchase those things.

Visit model homes for sale and imagine what changes you may make to your future home that you will be buying, then head to the car lot and sit in the car you will be driving in the near future.

All of this will be very important to manifesting these things. It's also important to fight any doubt that tries to creep in. Keeping your energy positive will begin the process of creating a new pattern in your mind that will be strong enough to overpower your old belief patterns. You must act and feel as though all of these things will one day be your reality and the universe is waiting for you to act on these things. If you can maintain this, you will achieve your IT, but it won't be easy. Every major life change or mind shift is difficult, but you must face it like a warrior. No matter what comes against you, no matter what or who confronts you, you will fight for the life you desire. You will climb to new levels on the PyramIT because you are worth it. You can become anything you choose to be and have anything you want and work for.

Often, we feel like we don't deserve success, wealth or health because early on we are taught that we aren't worthy, we owe something to society, or we have done bad stuff in our life. We believe we shouldn't want a better life, and should be satisfied with what we have, be grateful for where we are and never strive to be more.

This is not the law. You can become anything you choose and have anything you want. The universe doesn't care. It's easy to say, "I could never live a better life," or "I don't know what my purpose is." This way of thinking is common for average people, but you're not average. You have never been average. You've always known there was something special inside, you just didn't understand the steps to take you into a position to move up the PyramIT of purpose. Until you saw this book, you never understood there was a reason why you have continued to behave the way that you've behaved.

So once you attempt to move into this new direction, your mind will tell you it's not possible. You must acknowledge it, but you can't give into it. You just need to break the old way of thinking and utilize the unlimited power that lies within it and press on. This power you have is unlimited and the only limit to its power is the limits you place on it. You have unlimited and unemotional power. It will give you what you focus on, including negative or positive behaviors. This power doesn't discriminate. It will give you whatever you choose to believe is possible or impossible for your life. This power is the real you.

There is no negative or positive energy, there is only energy that is labeled negative or positive. When we can't see there was a lesson from an action or event and/or how it could help us in the future, it's labeled as negative. It would be more appropriate to call it high energy or low energy. This life is yours and only what you make of it. You must take responsibility for your own circumstances, which is why adversity is so important. It's through adversity that we learn valuable skills that help us become strong enough to handle life's challenges. The problem comes when we forget that we made it through former challenges, so when the next one hits, we forget we have the fortitude to make it through this challenge as well. There is nothing on this planet that we can't overcome if we utilize the energy that resides in us. The way to get over deep-rooted issues is by looking inside and seeing things the way they are, but not worse than they are. We then decide that if something is going to change, we must change it.

Look at your PyramIT when you wake up, in the afternoon, and before you head to bed. Meditate on what you want for your future. The system works if you are definite about what you want. Know that it will happen, and don't talk about it to others until it happens. Always act and think about it as though you already have it. Be open to the strange ways that may come to you to make it happen. You don't have to try to figure it all out, just believe your hard work will pay off. A farmer doesn't plant on Sunday and expect a full crop on Monday; he knows it will take time but it will be worth it, and you are worth it.

Try to keep your thoughts pure and only focus on things you want. Try not to focus on what you don't want because you tend to get whatever you focus on. If doubt attempts to creep in, don't allow it to stay for long; realize it is just your mind not understanding your intent to move to a new level because it is already comfortable where it is.

Everything around us has a living spirit, although some things may not express it in the same way. The more you become aware of the things around you and become aware of the power that everything possesses, the more you become aware of your ability to utilize this power.

As you become aware of your responsibility to walk in who you are, not who you were, the shift happens. If you want to lose weight or be healthier, you must be patient as exercise and eating better won't change 10, 20, or 30 years of eating terrible with no exercise. The same applies with our consciousness as it pertains to living a life of purpose. You can achieve your IT, but it takes time to break the old habits and the old way of thinking.

Start your list with a few modest requests at the beginning, just so you can see how powerful this tool is. This will be the start of your energy belief, and will help give you power to believe for things much larger, that you have always wanted deep within. You will develop a belief that these things can come true, and this will push you to the next level. In order to continue to achieve these new things, you must continue to believe you can change, and it is your choice to live your purpose. You will continue to have to work on your mind's doubt, and be sure to remind yourself that you've had success, you have enjoyed the feelings associated with success, it is possible for you to continue having that success, and you won't accept any energy that comes to convince you otherwise.

You can help yourself through the process of doubt by focusing on affirmative words, which you place at the top of your PyramIT. Think about the success you will have. Focus on the experiences you will have, the places you will go, the things you will buy, and the people that you will help.

Remember you deserve to have IT. You were born for IT, and it is who you are. Continue to meditate on this and when things get tough, as they most certainly will, you will be in control of what you chose to focus on.

When you wake up each morning, you create energy by deciding what your day will be like. You have control over your day—you've always had control—but in the past, we gave up this control to situations and experiences that happened the day before or what we were worried about. Make sure that before you leave the house you leave with the expectation of having a good day, regardless of what lies before you. Look at each person you interact with as a piece of your puzzle and their experiences are their experiences. They have nothing to do with what you will ultimately experience. You must overcome any negativity others may try to bring into your world. They are entitled to act with their feelings, and you are entitled to respond in a way that doesn't give up the power you created in order to have the day you create.

Realize that you have a shield around you, and the only way others can affect you is when you choose to go outside of your shield. Your shield will become stronger the more you stay in it and the more you learn the importance of not responding to the negativity of others. With your shield around you and a force inside you, when will you begin to act with this magnificent power to find your purpose and begin to live your IT? When you begin to see yourself as the person who you've yearned to become, you will feel a strong energy and your confidence will soar.

At first your change might not be noticeable, because the spark will shine on the inside of you, before fully shining on the outside. There is a goal inside all of us to be free and independent of the opinions of others, but many times we fall victim to wanting or needing approval from others. This conundrum is what many face and the key is deciding who you will make happy, you or them. Most people find it very difficult to make it to their purpose, because they are so reluctant to move away from their old lifestyles. It as if they live in a prison where the gates are unlocked, but they only see bars and never attempt to push the gate open. They also have such a great relationship with the other people who are locked in this prison, that they are reluctant to push open the unlocked gate.

Today we live in a world where our children are in need of people who are living their purpose, so we can help them break the cycle of negative behaviors and thinking.

God is light, God is energy, and this energy is inside all of us. To access this power, you must see God in you and since God is in you, you can control your life, not things outside of you. When you understand and really believe this, you will begin to utilize the energy available to you. You must internalize this energy inside to externally win against the challenges outside of you.

God will allow anyone to have what it is they believe they deserve they can have. God loves us because we are him and he is us. He can wish no harm to us, because he would be wishing harm to himself. God's relationship with us isn't about the emotions we will feel. His relationship with us is about consciousness. Being aware we can achieve whatever we focus on.

God accepts and loves us for who we are. He gives us a choice to become who we want to become, but he also loves us if we choose to remain the same. He respects us so much that he allows us to be less than who he has called us to become. The battle comes when we fight with ourselves, because we don't love who we are, we feel there is something else or someone else living within us, and it is that person who yearns to come out of hiding.

The success most people have in life isn't logical. It is the faith that regardless of where I've come from or what I've been through, I'm determined to make it happen. When we understand the Law of Attraction, we realize we are attracting what we want by focusing on whatever that is.

We can create thoughts through our power of thought, if our thoughts are strong about the thing we want. It will take time, but if we stay disciplined and committed it will happen.

If our family and friends have sucked us into their faulty belief system and are unwilling to believe that change is possible, we must disconnect from them. The people who win the battle of the mind, and disconnect from any limiting beliefs that they may have once possessed, are the people who go on to discover their purpose.

There is a part of us that struggles to hold on to the bottom of the PyramIT, because that's where most of our friends feel most comfortable. Yet there will be another part of you that will enjoy developing new beliefs and learning new information. This will be the struggle.

You will need to stay positive and keep climbing up the PyramIT, even though you will struggle with yourself. You must continue to focus on the positive energy inside of you to change your current status. You must overwhelm the negativity with positivity. Keep in mind that this negative energy has been in your mind for quite some time now, so it will be a fight to climb the PyramIT. It will fight you to stay where you are, because it has been comfortable there.

As you become more positive, you may feel lonely because people around you may stop wanting to be with you. The reality is that we are all connected to our previous tribe and this connection has also connected us to their dysfunctional ways.

Be prepared to learn to become comfortable receiving what it is you want, because it can and will come in different ways. When you begin to focus on this limitless energy that resides inside of you, you will become unstoppable in the things you will be able to receive. When we learn to develop the power inside discover our IT, then we are able to take our gifts and help others. It's when we choose the lesser self by becoming victims of circumstances and never developing our IT that the world suffers. We are truly powerful beings, but if we never discover our IT, we risk the chance of living a life less than the one that we were purposed to live.

I've found that people want to help others, but they aren't in a position to do so because they haven't helped themselves by discovering their true calling. A large part of receiving is giving, and when you become a giver, without expecting to receive, you will find that you will constantly receive, just based on your willingness to give.

The PyramIT of purpose, once understood, will help you become a more powerful person. It will help you recognize the true power that you possess.

Dr. D.F. Arnold

Day 8 — The Importance of Your Journey

Commit yourself to becoming more aware and more determined to learn from your journey. Get excited about learning from your mistakes and every day commit to creating the level of happiness you want. Our goals create our destiny! We must have enough compelling reasons to drive us forward to do whatever it takes to achieve our goals. What we're purposed to do is stronger than the results we receive. Who you become during the journey to achieving your goals is the real purpose.

Deon Sanders, a Hall of Fame football player, spoke about how all his life his goal was to go to the Super Bowl. When he made it to the Super Bowl for the first time and won, he found himself sitting in his hotel room soon after depressed, thinking, "Is that it?" He was focused on the results, when the real reward was in the journey.

When we move from focusing on results to enjoying and learning from the journey, we can find that everything good and bad was part of the plan to strengthen us to become the person needed to take on the next challenge. Our problems are there to strengthen us to handle our future. Your results are simply a byproduct of your journey.

Why do goals work? "As you think, so you become." If you develop a constant unwavering focus on something, you will experience it. When you set goals, you are making it known to your conscious and subconscious minds that where you are is not where you want to be. Having a goal creates positive forces that are necessary to move you forward.

Think about all of the things you will gain if you achieve your goals. Why are you committed to making these goals a reality? Make sure you link enjoyment to achieving it. Think about what you will continue to sacrifice if you don't achieve a goal. Link hurt to not achieving the goal. It is our desire that drives us and as Les Brown said, "You got to be hungry."

We have to be willing to admit that we are not happy with the way things are in our lives, and we would like them to be better. This will stir up that drive inside to help us create the changes that we want to see.

YOUR ASSIGNMENT:

1. Specific areas of my life that are not how I would like them to be:

_____

_____

_____

_____

_____

_____

2. In order for my life to be transformed, I have to consistently believe the following to be possible:

_____

_____

_____

_____

_____

_____

3. The list of beliefs I will hold in my mind to reach my ultimate goals are:

_____

_____

_____

_____

_____

_____

4. Things must change in my life and I know I
    can change them because:

_____

_____

_____

_____

_____

_____

Life has a way of making things you deal with
more and more challenging as you mature.
Therefore, you have probably handled a difficult
situation in the past and gotten through it. If you
haven't, this is it. So, as Nike would say, "Just Do
It!"

Day 9 — Your MFAs Shape Your Character

Your MFAs shape your character and destiny. If you are feeling any emotion, positive or negative, on a regular basis, it is the result of an internal ritual. Your rituals consist of the habitual ways you look at the world and how you talk to yourself.

1. List four negative MFAs you experience on a regular basis (i.e., discouragement, sadness).

2. Write down your rituals for each of these MFAs (i.e., what you must do in your mind in order to feel them).

3. List four positive MFAs you experience regularly.

4. Write down your rituals for each of these emotions.

Procrastination is nothing but a ritual. Here is how to overcome it:

1. Figure out what contributes to a ritual that you created.

2. If you don't do this, what will be the ultimate price you will have to pay?

3. If you had already gotten this done, how would your life be better? How much more joy would you have?

4. Develop the habit of saying: "I want to..." instead of "I have to..."

5. Develop the habit of moving your body to interrupt the pattern of procrastination.

YOUR ASSIGNMENT:

1. A pattern interruption for each of my four negative MFAs would be:

_____
_____
_____
_____
_____
_____

2. A trigger for my positive MFAs would be:

_____
_____
_____
_____

_____

_____

3. I get myself into the ritual of procrastination by
_____ and I will try to break out of it by
_____.

_____

_____

_____

_____

_____

_____

Dr. D.F. Arnold

Day 10 — Attaching

Whenever your MFAs get into a state that has its complete focus, anything that consistently happens around you while you are in this state gets associated with it.

This process is called "attaching." For example, there might be a song that reminds you of a person you once dated and whenever you hear that song, you think of that person. That's because while you were in that emotional state, the unique sound of that song was in the background. This music was linked or associated in your mind with that person and that situation, so any time you hear that particular song you remember some of those specific feelings again.

We are always attaching. We consistently associate and create meanings out of what has happened and is happening to us at any particular time. This is usually all happening unconsciously. The secret is to understand this concept of attaching in order to help us take conscious control of this process and use it to condition ourselves to feel and act the way we would like for our new ideal self in any given situation.

Wouldn't it be useful to attach yourself to feel good about any situation that you don't necessarily enjoy, like going to that boring class? Or to get rid of the negative attachments that you may have to it? If you gain control or master this skill, you can change virtually any area of your life.

How are positive attachments created? This process has been done to you for years by advertisers. Think of one of your favorite jingles or songs of a particular brand, and you will notice it's impossible to think of just the song without thinking of the brand. Therefore, if you are in a grocery store and trying to figure out which product to buy, your mind will go to the commercial about that product and then you may buy it. Without consciously realizing it, your mind has been conditioned to buy that product by the visual remembrance of that commercial.

Here is how to create a series of positive attachments:

1. Close your eyes, identify the behavior you want to change, and imagine the behavior in your mind.

2. Create a new picture of yourself and how you would act and feel if you made the desired changes.

3. The key to this pattern is repetition and changing your MFAs when you are in this new emotional state. You have to feel good about the new you and your new MFAs. Do this five or six times, as focused as you can, and have fun doing it! What you're telling your brain is, "Do this..." until the old picture automatically triggers the new picture, new MFAs, and thus new behavior.

YOUR ASSIGNMENT:

1. Create new positive attachments.

   a. Close your eyes and take yourself back to a time when you really felt happy.

   b. Keep concentrating on that feeling. Those are the feelings you will immediately think of the moment your MFAs take a negative turn. The key is to have several of these positive thoughts that you can access, and do it over and over until you can trigger the feeling without any negative attachments.

2. Try to have at least seven positive emotions at
   your fingertips. List them.

_____

_____

_____

_____

_____

_____

Days 11-14 — Attaching Financial Success

Once you understand that money is only a means to measure the exchange of value between people, you will change your thoughts on the process of acquiring it.

Seven reasons most people never make it financially:

1. They associate negative thoughts with making and/or having money.

2. They never turn having an abundance of money into an absolute must.

3. They never develop an effective strategy for building wealth.

4. They fail to follow through consistently on their financial plan.

5. They rely too much on "experts."

6. They become financially complacent.

7. They allow financial crisis to turn into financial ruin.

To condition yourself for wealth, you must develop strategies for:

1. Attracting money into your life.

2. Managing your money.

3. Sharing your money with others, which will give you tremendous joy.

To master these strategies, use modeling.

1. Find people who are getting these results and study what they do. Even if that person isn't in your life, with technology you can read about a plethora of individuals that started in dire straits, picked themselves up, and are now living the life most would dream of having.

2. If you commit to doing the same things consistently, you will get the same results. Give yourself a financial checkup so you can "heal" yourself quickly.

3. What limits you from believing you can have absolute financial abundance? What have you associated in the past with having financial excess?

You will find financial abundance is excess, having more than enough. Many people will associate negative MFAs to this and wonder why they never maintain a financial position of "excess dollars."

It's impossible to have an excess of anything you don't truly believe in.

4. Ask yourself if there is an amount of money that represents financial abundance? Have you made this number a must for your life? Or have you gotten comfortable and your current must is only the ability to live comfortably by paying your current bills?

If you have not established a specific number, do so and commit to having it.

5. Today, do something toward developing a financial plan. Remember, after every thought an action toward the thought is what moves you closer to it.

Contact a financial planner, find a mentor (one who is doing some great things that you would like to see happen in your life), and read a book on creating wealth. Someone has made what you dream of having a reality.

6. If you have honestly began taking action, you must start believing that you are making financial progress. It could be that you have simply made up your mind that you are no longer going to spend money every time you go into a store. Taking action toward financial progress means you have made a decision that the best investment is yourself. Maybe it's a decision you are going to make about what to believe about financial excess. Every small action leads to a pattern of habits, which ultimately can be used to create the financial freedom you truly deserve.

7. Make a list of the things you have heard about money and don't fully understand. Make a committed decision to find the people who can give you the answers you need. The problem is not that you don't know, the problem is that you're not asking someone who does.

8. Write a paragraph about why you are going to continue to follow through and avoid complacency. What were the excuses you used in the past?

You must believe that the fear that has stopped you up to this point is nothing but a temporary setback that had many   lessons to learn from, and move on to the life you truly deserve. Write down a couple of situations where you thought there was no way out, but you got through it. Use this to remind yourself of the capacity you have to turn challenges into opportunities.

YOUR ASSIGNMENT:

1. What limits me from believing that I can have absolute financial abundance?

_____

_____

_____

_____

_____

_____

2. What specific amount of money will I need to represent financial abundance to me?

_____

_____

_____

_____

_____

_____

3. What will I commit to doing today toward developing a financial plan?

_____

_____

_____

_____

_____

_____

4. What did I learn today to help me make progress?

_____

_____

_____

_____

_____

_____

5. Aspects of personal finance that I don't understand.

_____

_____

_____

_____

_____

_____

6. Why I must be committed to follow through.

_____

_____

_____

_____

_____

_____

7. Write down a couple of situations where you thought there was no way out, but you got through it.

_____

_____

_____

_____

_____

_____

In any situation where you sabotage yourself, especially financially, it's because you believe on some level the accumulation of money is going to lead to more hurt than enjoyment.

To begin attracting wealth you must:

1. Realize you are already wealthy.

2. Believe that what you are creating will also allow others to fulfill their dreams.

To eliminate financial self-sabotage, this is what must happen:

1. Write a description of all of the hurt you have experienced because you haven't had the financial abundance you deserve.

2. When you think of money, what words come to your mind? Make a list.

3. What things have you been told about money, starting in childhood? Write them down.

4. If money was not an issue and you had an abundance of it, write down how your life would be better.

5. Remove your limiting beliefs about money and begin attaching new ones by laughing at the old ones.

Write down this information and repeat it to yourself over and over again.

Beliefs that will empower and will lead you to financial freedom:

1. When I continually give to others, the more money I will receive on an ongoing, consistent basis.

2. I must live in an attitude of gratitude and I must give much more to others than I expect to receive back.

Financial abundance comes from doing what you love doing and making sure it creates tremendous value for other people.

To find the appropriate vehicle for you to build wealth, answer the following questions:

1. What do you love to do?

2. How could you do this to benefit others so they would be willing to invest in it?

3. How could you do it to reach a multitude of people?

4. How could you offer it as a service?

YOUR ASSIGNMENT:

Every day for the next 21 days, write down an idea for increasing your income, or ways in which you could earn more from the income you already have.

Doing this for 21 days will break old habits of lazy thoughts and begin to train your mind to look for economic opportunities. They are all around you, but you must develop a new mindset that notices them and causes you to act upon them.

Day 15 — Eliminating Fears

To eliminate fears, we must change the way we look at fear and success. First, create definitions of what must happen for you to feel successful and to feel like a failure. To remove fear of failure, decide you are going to be free of this fear, and then interrupt your past pattern.

1. Get yourself into a strong, positive state and create a positive attachment.

2. Imagine you are at a movie theater and the show that is playing is one of your past failures. Imagine it exactly the way it happened and as if it was happening at that moment.

3. With a smile, run the entire memory in reverse at high speed.

4. Now run it forward twice as fast to the end and stop.

5. Run it backward and forward repeatedly as fast as you can, each time making it more bizarre.

6. Now think about the painful memory. You should be smiling!

Finally, imagine having the success you want over and over again until it is real for you and becomes a sense of certainty that is emotionally conditioned.

YOUR ASSIGNMENT:

1. To eliminate the fear of success, you must turn the fear of hurt on itself. Take a moment and write down all you will lose if you don't remove the fear of success. What will it cost if you keep indulging in this emotion?

_____

_____

_____

_____

_____

_____

2. What will you gain by overcoming this fear of success?

_____

_____

_____

_____

_____

_____

3. Close your eyes and imagine yourself feeling free from the fear once and for all.

   To overcome fear of rejection this is what must happen:

_____

_____

_____

_____

_____

_____

4. Make a decision that you are through allowing it to control your life.

   Get enough leverage to follow through. Write down the cost of not overcoming this fear and the benefits of being free of it.

_____

_____

_____

_____

_____

_____

5. Create a new set of rules for what must happen for you to feel rejected.

   Close your eyes once again and begin to interrupt your old pattern.

   Create a strong positive attachment, and then fire it off as you imagine yourself being rejected.

   Write down two experiences when you felt you failed and two when you felt rejected, and think about what you learned from each experience.

_____

_____

_____

_____

_____

_____

Day 16 — Sabotaging Your Dreams

In all actuality, everything we engage in, including self-sabotage, we do with positive intent. Through its actions, our brain at some level, conscious or unconscious, is always trying to benefit us.

An example of this might be if you consistently pull back right before you are about to have a great success. This is not your brain trying to hurt you. If fact, it may be trying to protect you from a situation where you may ultimately feel rejected. It's important to realize that your brains' intent is good. Your brain is on your side. You simply need to condition it to be more effective.

What's happening when we begin to sabotage ourselves is that we have mixed MFAs. That is, we associate both hurt and enjoyment to the same outcome. For example, some individuals have been in intimate relationships that were quite painful. Now they find themselves moving toward relationships out of the desire to have intimacy, love, and connection, but at certain points they pull back because they associate the hurt of the past and the fear of rejection with all of their relationships.

YOUR ASSIGNMENT

1. Identify any tendencies you may have to sabotage yourself.

_____

_____

_____

_____

_____

_____

2. Feel good because your brain is trying to help you avoid hurt and gain enjoyment.

3. Get control to make a change.

4. Interrupt the old pattern.

5. Rehearse achieving the success you want and feel the pleasure of succeeding until the new pattern is conditioned.

There are two primary ways you can create self-confidence at any moment:

1. Control your mental focus. The fastest way to change what you are focusing on is to change the questions you are asking yourself. Change

from, "What happens if I fail at this?" or, "Why do I always screw these things up?" to, "What's the best way to get this done now?" or, better yet, "What's the best way to get this done and enjoy the process?"

2. Change your core beliefs. Change from, "I've never done it before so I don't see how I could do it today," to, "If I can dream it, I can achieve it."

The success statement is similar to a mathematical equation. We learned in school that anything multiplied by zero will equal zero, and this is the same for our dreams and desires. Any dream multiplied by doubt or fear will cancel out our desire and leave us with nothing.

D (dream) x D (doubt) or F (fear) = 0 (nothing)

To have more confidence, change your focus from yourself to how you can contribute to others.

YOUR ASSIGNMENT:

1. Recall seven of your greatest successes and write a sentence or two describing each one. Use these examples to remind yourself that your mind will always find a way!

Dr. D.F. Arnold

_____

_____

_____

_____

_____

_____

Relationships

Everything that has happened in your life can work for your benefit if you let it. Had you not been through those situations you wouldn't have the narrative needed to help others, and the expertise needed to understand that life is a series of tests given to us as pop quizzes, to see if we have learned from our experiences.

The PyramIT of Purpose is what you need to understand in order to determine what's been holding you back, and to now recognize what's possible, if you believe that you deserve IT. Your PyramIT will give you the tools to change what has been impossible in your past, to now create new thoughts, energy, and relationships for an improved future.

It is my hope that with this information you can become the person you were created to be. I want everyone who looks at the PyramIT of Purpose to recognize they have the power to create the life they truly deserve, they can go deeper and live higher.

The smallest areas of our behavior we choose to change can spark something that can change the world. Like a fire that starts with a spark can ruin a whole community, a positive spark in your mind can have the opposite affect and change the community for the better.

The most important lesson you will learn from relationships with yourself and others is the lesson of forgiveness. How, who, and when we forgive will be one the most important relationships we will have. We can only receive what we give, and once we begin giving, the universe has a way of letting us receive that from which we weren't even expecting. People will hurt our feelings, and we will hold things against them because of the actions they exhibit toward us.

It's only when we forgive that we don't retain the anger. If we hang on to the hurt it keeps us in bondage. Some of us still hold anger against someone in high school, but the unfortunate part is that you're still hanging on to past experiences. Many times, we won't forgive because we're so angry and this anger continues to hurt us, not the other person. This lack of forgiveness and anger controls your behaviors and actions over the years and literally lives in your mind. This then stops you from living your life free from friction. It's friction with yourself and others that will never allow you to discover your IT, because your IT can't be all it was designed to be if there is turmoil and dysfunction.

We hold onto our failures by holding onto mistakes. We must forgive ourselves from wrong thinking and past relationships. Forgiveness allows you to control what used to control you. It allows you to determine what you allow to have access to your power. It is this power that is found in your choices.

The universe is unemotional, meaning it doesn't care who discovers their IT, only that they really want IT. The universe is pure energy. It will accept whatever thoughts or ideas that you project, and will reflect them back to you, the same way a mirror projects your image.

For years, we thought that in order to have certain things we had to act a certain way. This isn't the case, and we have seen this happen with a number of people. It's all about the energy that is projected toward the IT. Once this energy is established, nothing can stop it from happening.

This energy will give you anything you believe in, no more and no less. The key to understanding this is to look at your current beliefs, thoughts and feelings. When we entered this world, our thoughts, feelings, and ideas were limitless because our minds were clean slates. They were canvases with nothing on them, free to be marked with the images we create. We have a free will that isn't subject to the thoughts and ideas that others place upon us, about who and what they think we should be.

As kids we often attempted what adults saw as impossible or crazy because kids aren't yet aware of boundaries and limitations. They will jump off the highest hill with no regard to the fact that they may get hurt. These limitations have forced your IT to drift further and further into darkness. Though still inside you, your IT becomes more difficult to locate. The new education that you have discovered about what is safe and what isn't starts the journey of believing in the impossible instead of continuing to believe in what is possible, if you just didn't give up on your IT. The impossible is just an illusion formed by faulty belief patterns we develop from the experiences of others or the experiences of our own failures. This faulty belief pattern in many cases has been passed down from generations to generations of people in your family who failed to continue disrupting the failure pattern and instead gave up and gave in to this way of thinking and allowed it to control the gift (life) they were given. The first failure of that family member or friend gained power as it continued to develop like the snowball that turned into the avalanche that destroyed the town.

Once this snowball gets rolling and the future generation believe this is their lot in life based on the generational thought process, then this way of thinking because rigid and unwilling to bend to believe there may be another way. And now since these are the people who teach us what we can or can't do, we become subject to believe what they say is true about our future. This belief system is planted inside us and now grows as it is watered by other adults who think alike. This doesn't allow our IT inside us to shine. You see our IT can never shine when we become locked into rigidity and doesn't allow for the genius of our IT to shine.

We all have a mission.

Most of us can't achieve our highest self and discover our IT because we're locked within the confines and prisons that our family and friends created for us.

We are more than this shell we our currently housed in; we are an infinite being with the power of the highest inside us. Your IT is yearning to be released to provide you with a way of life that you are currently living so far beneath.

We all had a seed planted in us from conception. We were born to this higher self, this higher power and we all knew what our IT was. Unfortunately, our brain wasn't developed enough to coherently express our IT.

The problem is we no longer remember what our IT was as we have allowed people, life and our environment to trick us out of the ability to access it. This great power that we have is lying dormant inside of us, waiting to be released.

We all have a heroic mission we are on and the plan is and always will be for us to discover this mission, but unfortunately many of us never will.

We aren't taught the power of our purpose and we aren't taught the power that comes from realizing our IT and acting in our highest power.

Everything you've been through, the good experiences and the perceived bad or unwanted experiences, were all necessary for your journey. Those experiences provided you with what you needed to conquer in order to pass your test.

Your mind only started recording this life's journey the day you were born, but that seed that was planted inside of you will lay dormant until you start to understand your life has a purpose. At the early age of adolescent you won't understand this journey or this mission, but deep inside it has always been there waiting for you to tap into it.

Many people wonder why it is so hard to discover their IT. It's not. The only hard part about discovering your IT is deciding it's time to live at a higher level than you are currently operating.

Motional speaker Les Brown once said that the easiest thing he does is make a million dollars, but the hardest thing that he dealt with was believing he could do it. That's what we all deal with, our minds fighting through the faulty conversations and training telling us what's not possible. As discussed earlier in the chapter, we have a tendency to believe that which is untrue.

Some people will be okay staying where they are. Some will choose to stay there, while others will believe they are stuck or destined to stay in that same place. The same decision that others had to make to become unstuck, is the same decision or choice we all possess to do or be something other than what we are currently doing or being.

Some remain stuck because they make their problems bigger than their potential to become unstuck. There is no mountain too big for us to climb. Similarly, there is no problem that can't be solved. It just may require you to solve it with different information than what was used to create it.

The biggest thing that separates those who overcome their problems from those that don't is they <u>believe</u> it's possible for them to overcome any obstacle. They won't let the mountains of fear and doubt overtake what they know they can beat.

If you keep learning all the time, you have a huge advantage. People say they want to learn, but they tend to wait to do it someday instead of today.

We must have a broad vision of what our life must become in order to live the life we deserve. The reason why successful people always talk about writing your vision down is simple: They do this because when things get hard, which they will, they go back to those pictures, to their mission, and they think of the reasons why they started. Those people picture what their lives would be like if they didn't achieve their IT, and that becomes harder than the mirage in front of them.

You must create a connection of compelling reason why it must happen in order for your dreams to come true. You must see it and imagine it happening.

If you want to become a good student in school, you must attach what becoming a good student means for your ultimate goals in life. If biology isn't your thing, that's okay, but failing biology isn't okay. The thing you to do is work hard to pass biology and attach the pain associated with not passing it to motivate you. Until we know what we want our lives to be, we will never be able to do the things necessary to have the lives and experiences we deserve. Success isn't free, and if you're not willing to pay the price, you will never be successful.

The most expensive cost of success is time. Every successful person will tell you that this is one of the most difficult, but gratifying, parts of success. This is what will separate those who kind-of want it, from those who really want it. Unsuccessful people look at the clock for time. They believe success moves in a circle, so if they don't do it today, they can just do it tomorrow. Successful people view time as linear, in a straight line, so they realize that if they don't get it done at that moment, they just wasted one of the most valuable resource they possess.

Successful people understand the importance of developing the knowledge and skills to go to the next level. It will save you time if you realize the importance of modeling or researching someone who is doing what you're interested in. This will save you that most valuable resource (time), and this is the fastest way to learn. Why reinvent a wheel that has already been invented? Successful people talk about the importance of reading, learning in the areas that interest them, and using that information as an opportunity for transformation.

After you acquire the skills necessary to transform the areas in your life you want to change, you have to practice it over and over until it becomes a habit. It's important to stay disciplined enough to follow through and resist the temptations to revert back to old mindsets filled with old behaviors that exchange faith for doubt. You can stay disciplined enough to not fall back into negative behaviors by having daily conversations and being fully emerged into the new you. This new you is passionate about discovering your IT at whatever cost.

If you want to learn a new language or play the piano, you won't learn it by doing it once a month. Your emergence into your PyramIT of Purpose must be consistent. You must live and breathe your PyramIT.

For example, personal development is my life. I watch at least three videos a day on it and I'm reading a book a month on it. That's where this PyramIT of Purpose system came from. I knew I had information from my experiences that could help others change their worlds. I'm dedicated to this. I knew if I could change my relationships, words and thoughts, I could change my life. It was so important to me that I became committed to my IT. Everyday, I'm learning something that can further my personal growth and can help others grow further than they ever thought possible. If you aren't learning something every day that can help you grow, then you are dying a slow death to things that are stealing the life you deserve. If you're not growing, you're dying. If you're not managing your time to learn and grow, you're mismanaging your time. If you're not taking time to master the things you are passionate about, then you can never live the life you deserve. Your life can only be full when you are living your"PURPOSE". The reason so many people experience this is because they have sacrificed passion for inaction and have made excuses for what could be advantages and labeled them as disadvantages. They've allowed dysfunction to become the main function in their lives.

Your heart and "PURPOSE" are attached to the power you possess inside of you to change the lives of others. Most people have a disconnect with what they could/should be trying to master. They have a disconnection from their IT. Try to work on something each day that moves you toward your IT. If you want to become good or the best at anything, you need to work at it. Some of this work will require you to find a coach or a mentor who can hold you accountable to become the person you would like to become. This person will give you feedback and encourage you when you are falling below the level you told them you would like to move toward. This person can also hold you accountable to the deadlines you have created to move to a new level.

You must remain focused, because the pressure will come to break you. It will attempt to move you back down the PyramiIT to that dysfunctional place you have made comfortable for many years. It will welcome you back with open arms and it will try to convince you that you are missing out on something.

Dysfunction loves company, and it loves to distort what's real. Remember what's real is that which can't be explained. That's why human beings are so complex, because the complexities of the human experience takes many turns. We learn, we fall and we learn all over again. We grow and expand and then we shrink to unthinkable depths. It's during these experiences that we question our existence. We question what it is about us that prevents us from moving to the level we know we would like to be at, but ultimately sacrifice that level for a level of discomfort that we make comfortable.

Relationships help you learn about yourself and help you discover what your purpose is. Although we come into this world by ourselves and will leave this world by ourselves, it is the relationships we develop while on this planet that help us to understand our purpose.

For years we have operated under the assumption that because we've made mistakes or have done things that have caused us to fail or fall, we don't deserve to have success or live our purpose. Due to this thinking, we have allowed our past mistakes to paralyze us and keep us from reaching our IT. We think God or the universe has given us a bad deck of cards to play with so we refuse to play the game.

God or the Universe has no respect of person. Choosing to be rich, or choosing to be successful is a choice that each individual has the choice to make. The infinite power that resides in us gives us the ability to be whatever we make the choice to be. We are free to choose our Life.

We must be specific and focused on what it is we want. If we say we want more money and we find a penny on the ground we have gotten exactly what we have asked for. The reality is to manifest the things we want and the life we want to live is that easy. There is an abundance of everything we would like in our warehouse and all we need to do is Ask, Seek and Knock on the door, go in and pick it up.

An example of being specific is, I would like a 2015 or newer car by the end of the year. I will work every day and stay focused on obtaining my car until I receive it. You can't be confused or have any type of indecision when it comes to your purpose. You must Discover IT. Develop IT. LIVE IT. After all, if you can't describe IT, who can?

Once you stop complicating things in your life, you will discover that things will come to you without having to force it. For you to reach your purpose, you may not understand how, you must only understand why it is important for you to achieve this purpose. You maintain your power at all times and you make a decision to never give away this power to people, problems or circumstances.

Remember there is no time as you live in a state of now. Feel yourself living the life you want to live now. You are at the top of the PyramIT, living your IT. You are there, you have IT already. You have defeated what has defeated you in the past. You have changed yourself into the person who has always lived inside you. You are a positive individual and all the events that happen today are happening for you to live your highest power.

Dr. D.F. Arnold

Day 17 — Relationships

One of the biggest things that keep people from having the relationships they want is because they tend to look for a relationship, or someone, to be the solution to their problems. In a relationship, this approach will be disempowering to both parties. A relationship must be seen as a place to give, rather than a place to get.

Your relationship will fail primarily because of the following:

1. The laws of familiarity and passion   decrease, then negative "weights" are formed, which are the primary killers of relationships.

   a. To prevent negative weights, make sure you are not focusing on the other person when you are having negative MFAs.

   b. Keep control by not allowing arguments to get out of control, try to interrupt patterns with each other. Be playful!

2. We fail to consistently meet the strategies of love and attraction of our partner. We all have

unique triggers or weights that cause us to feel love and attraction.

a. Some of us feel loved through the actions of our partner and they need to be *shown* they are loved, i.e., we want someone to look at us with a loving look or take us places to show they love us, or maybe even buy us things.

b. Some people need to hear they are loved in a specific way with a certain tone of voice.

c. Some people need to be touched in a certain way. Some need a gentle touch, some need to be held tightly so they know their partner passionately cares.

Everyone is different. Everyone is unique. You must know the strategy of your partner.

If you want your relationships to last, you must do the following:

1. Find out what makes the person feel loved and do it consistently.

2. Give to that person what you most want to receive; don't get trapped in the, "You do it first, and then I will reciprocate" trend.

a. Use passion to enhance the quality of your relationship.

b. Ask questions that encourage love to be expressed.

c. Be spontaneous—work at creating moments that are etched in the other person's mind.

Your relationship can only work by remaining committed to doing the extra.

You cannot create anything sustainable without being committed.

YOUR ASSIGNMENT:

1. What I want and don't want in a relationship are:

_____

_____

_____

_____

_____

_____

2. In order for me to be happy and contribute in an effective way, my relationship needs:

_____

_____

_____

_____

_____

_____

3. With your partner, develop a list of unique things you can do together to enhance your relationship on an ongoing basis. Special things we can do together to enhance our relationship are:

_____

_____

_____

_____

_____

_____

Day 18 — Problem Solving

In order to effectively solve problems, you must do the following:

1. Manage your MFAs. Learn to associate massive hurt to anything that causes you discourse and associate joy to solving the problem.

2. Write your problems out in your journal. Spend no more than 20% of the time defining it. Eighty percent of your time should be spent on finding solutions.

3. Come up with your best plan for handling each challenge and act upon it as quickly as possible. Immediate action is the key.

4. Notice what you are getting from the current actions you have been exhibiting.

5. If what you are doing isn't working, it's time to change your approach. Be more flexible by asking yourself, "What would happen if..."

6. Look for role models and seek their guidance.

7. Try to look at your problems as challenges and opportunities for you to grow.

Use the following problem-solving questions to put yourself in a positive, resourceful state for finding effective solutions.

PROBLEM-SOLVING QUESTIONS

1. What makes this problem different from others I have overcome in the past?

2. What steps am I willing to take to make it the way I want?

3. What will I give up in order to make it the way I want?

4. How can I enjoy the journey while I am taking action steps to make it the way I want?

YOUR ASSIGNMENT:

1. Using a problem you currently have, go through the four questions and use the space below to respond:

_____

_____

_____

_____

_____

_____

Dr. D.F. Arnold

Day 19 — Life Statements

Confidence

1. I have the ability to do whatever it takes to succeed, and if I get stuck, I can find whatever resource is needed for me to succeed.

2. I am learning from my journey and I enjoy the challenges life brings.

3. When I get up in the morning, I am passionate, powerful, and ready to go!

4. I feel healthy, strong, and excited about life.

5. I am very confident with everything that I am selected to do because I have talents that are waiting to be used.

6. I am a master at everything that challenges me.

7. I have deep respect for everyone I encounter each day.

8. Excellence is not my goal, it is my expectation.

9. I easily forgive others, just as easily as I forgive myself.

10. My confidence is unshakable because I know I can do whatever I make a committed decision to do.

Respecting your temple

1. I respect my temple and take excellent care of it each day.

2. I think healthy thoughts.

3. I eat and drink only good foods and beverages.

4. I wake up each day feeling great.

5. I have an abundance of energy.

6. I will always feel and look young and healthy.

7. I have the energy necessary for all that I want to do.

8. I retire each night feeling grateful for my day.

Financial Success

1. I was born to give freely from the abundance that I have been blessed with.

2. I have so much to give that I am able to share it freely with others each day.

3. My work helps others, and I am richly rewarded.

4. I attract more financial abundance each day.

5. I am a giver and what I give comes back tenfold.

6. I am grateful for the great abundance in my life.

7. I experience all of the wealth that surrounds me every day.

8. The wealth of my creator circulates throughout my life—His wealth flows to me in abundance.

9. I feel prosperous and I think prosperous thoughts.

10. I handle and invest my money wisely, and I profit daily.

Action!

1. I receive joy from using my personal power to benefit others and myself.

2. I feel great joy as I take action to accomplish my goals.

3. I am in the habit of taking action.

4. I am not lazy and I make the most out of my time each day.

5. I am in control of my destiny.

6. I take action immediately, and I make my time serve me.

7. I am eager to wake up and get started.

8. I take consistent action to accomplish my purpose.

9. I feel grateful for the abundance I enjoy.

10. I enjoy achieving my dreams.

Understanding the PyramIT of Purpose

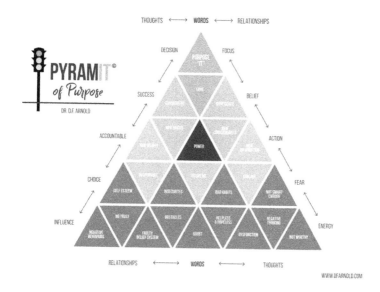

The secret to understanding the PyramIT of Purpose is not using will power. The secret is to know and face the truth. You must know and face the truth about yourself if you want to change. Nothing will change in your life until you face the truth about your weaknesses, your relationships, your failures, your past and future.

Your choices are far more powerful than your circumstances. You may not like how complicated your life has become. But with few exceptions, no one is forcing you to keep your life complicated. You have the power to simplify your life. In fact, to realize your Purpose, you must assume responsibility for your life and carefully choose how you will spend your time.

It's necessary to learn your truth before anything can change in your life. Here's why: Behind every self-defeating habit in your life is a lie that you continue to believe. If you get in debt, "I can always pay it back." You might have overestimated how much you were going to make, or you believed the lie that you needed a better car. But do you? Are you sure it's the truth? Can you prove it's the truth? Are you absolutely certain that what you believe you've said about your finances is true? What about your relationships? What about the things you say to yourself about yourself? Is the way you think about your past or about some event the truth?

Personal change starts with understanding that you were created with a Purpose and for a PURPOSE.

The PyramIT of Purpose

What you hear from friends, family on television or read in books isn't always going to help you, because it's not always the truth. The PyramIT of Purpose will show you how to get back to the life you were created to live, and it will show you how to remain on the path to your Purpose.

As long as you build your life on a foundation of lies, misconceptions, deceptions, or half-truths, you will never discover your PURPOSE. But when you face the truth and respond to the truth, you will begin to see change in your life.

Change requires making choices. It's not enough to dream of changing. It's not enough to desire change. In order for you to change, you will need to make a decision. You must choose to change. Change is intentional. Are you going to be any different in six months? Are you going to be better a year from now? Are you going to be healthier, stronger and more mature? Are you going to be happier? Are you going to be less in debt? I can tell you the answer right now: It will only happen if you choose to change, because it isn't going to happen accidentally.

It requires a choice. We have to make intentional choices in order to discover our Purpose, which means we must let go of some old things in order to grab hold of some new things.

Some of us get stuck in the middle, and we tend to fail because we aren't willing to let go of doubt, old habits, and the old ways of thinking. You have to let go of your old ways. If you want to have lasting change and pursue your Purpose, you MUST refocus your mind.

Specifically, you need to change your thought patterns from focusing on what you don't want to focus on to what you *do* want to focus on. Because whatever you focus on is what you move toward.

Here's the secret to changing your Focus: Don't fight it. Just refocus. Whatever you resist persists. It's time to change your focus.

Whatever gets your attention gets you. When you focus on your Purpose it will keep you from getting distracted. Why? Because if you're thinking about what you were created for, you're not thinking about things that are not as important.

It's true in every single area of life good or bad. If you focus on the green area of the PyramIT, it's going to pull you that direction. If you focus on the words at the bottom of the PyramIT, they're going to pull you that direction. Whatever you focus on gets your attention. Whatever gets your attention is going to get you. The key is to just change your focus. As you strive to reach your Purpose, it's important to remember that life on Earth is just a temporary assignment. Knowing this truth should radically alter your values and fix your attention on more important things.

The words at the bottom of the PyramIT follow a predictable pattern: attention, arousal, and action. Your mind gets hooked, your mind kicks in, and then you act on it.

If you're serious about breaking free from living a life that is below the level that you are capable of living, let me be very blunt with you: You will never do it without support. You will never do it on your own. This system is guaranteed to help you break away from the life you no longer chose to live.

In fact, once you understand the PyramIT of Purpose, you'll see how it will begin transforming your life and lives of others around you.

All of us at one time or another deal with the disempowering words found at the bottom of the PyramIT. It is a myth to think that you're never going to get to a point in your life where you're not influenced by negative people, situations, or things.

You can't always control your circumstances, and many times you won't be able to control the way you feel. But you can control what you think about. That's always your choice. However, if you change the way you think, it changes the way you feel, and that will change the way you act.

The way you respond to someone or to a situation is definitely going to affect your future. If you respond correctly and you do the right thing, even when you don't feel like it, it pays great dividends in the future.

We face things that try to distract us from our Purpose every day. It's a battle that takes place inside us and that makes us vulnerable, particularly if we don't know how to fight it. One of the reasons we so often walk around discouraged and defeated is because we don't understand that we're in a battle for our Purpose.

The PyramIT of Purpose

The enemy is constantly battling for your mind and your Purpose. That's where the battle happens. When you receive an idea, it's inspiration, but the enemy will attempt to distract you through temptation. You have the ability to choose every day which thought you're going to dwell on.

These three things will help you change any negative disempowering thoughts, and cause you to move up the PyramIT.

1. Responsibility

2. Discipline

3. Control

Responsibility is the first step: *Accept that it happened.* What does acceptance do? It allows you to take the power from, what used to have power over you, and that's where the battle is going on. The truth is that we bring most of our problems on ourselves. We just need to accept responsibility and quit blaming others. Every time we blame somebody else, we must wait for them to solve the problem, and if they are unwilling to solve it, we become stuck, waiting for them to give us something that they may be unable or unwilling to give us.

The second step, even before you can say "I'm responsible", you have to learn to say "I control my emotions". You must recognize that you have the power to defeat any limiting belief. Your problems aren't afraid of you, but they do dissipate from a controlled mind. The PyramIT of Purpose becomes a weapon when you memorize it. The number one reason you're under stress is because you're in conflict with Purpose. You're trying to control things that you can't control. You can't control your husband or your kids or your wife or your job or your future or your past or any of that stuff. The more you do it, the more you will be out of harmony with your true calling, and that puts you in opposition and not only will you continue losing this conflict, but you're also going to be tired.

Without a doubt, the single most effective tool to combating negative thoughts, is to remain focused and exercise discipline. If you don't discipline yourself when it comes to the things that used to throw you off track, you'll have no traction to move up the PyramIT. Every day, you have to decide who or what's going to be in control of your life. Have you noticed that the moment you establish a goal in your life, you start hearing people say, "Who do you think you are?" or "It can't be done" or "Forget about it"? The antidote to the voices of doubt is to instead listen to people who have made it to the top of their PyramIT.

Most successful people listened to their inner voice directing them to their Purpose. They didn't ignore the warnings that their world would be destroyed, if they kept associating with that group of people, or continued doing that certain thing. They chose to believe, what they had not yet seen. That's what faith is — being certain of something we don't see. We were created for a Purpose, and some people may think it's pretty crazy. But you've got to stay focused on what you know and live a life of purpose, and you'll have the adventure of a lifetime!

There are countless laws that impact our lives and daily actions. But there are other laws just waiting to be discovered and put to work from within; laws that anyone can use to live a limitless and prosperous life.

It is our decisions that shape our destiny. To access your "PURPOSE" using the PyramIT, you must first make a choice to change what you once thought was impossible, and begin to believe that it's not only possible to live the life that you deserve, but it is necessary. This system will change your life.

It starts with believing you have a choice to change what you once thought was impossible, into what you now believe can be possible.

Change: Your life changes when you make a decision to change the choices you have made in the past. Those choices have ultimately affected your future up to this point.

Impossible: Some people have trouble visualizing or imagining what their life could be because their mind only wants to focus on the reality of the way things currently are. We must develop our imaginations to create the life we deserve because this ability allows us to change our world. We can develop this by doing numerous little things, including allowing ourselves a couple of minutes each day to let go and fantasize about what it would be like to live that life. This can awaken us to power and the passion to pursue our IT.

Possible: Anything is possible. The process to change can look simple, but what can be most difficult is deciding that enough is enough and it's time for you to change. If we use our imaginations to stimulate beliefs that we have what we want before everyone else sees it, then we are already on the right track to achieving what is possible.

The foundation of the PyramIT is grounded in three things:

- Relationships

- Words

- Thoughts

Relationships: The relationships that we have with others and, more importantly, with ourselves will be important to understand in order to live your purpose.

Words: We must use our brains to think, and in doing so, we must create new narratives of how we will live our lives. The conversations we have with ourselves and with others should be abundant and full of faith. Try not to complain around others; instead, evaluate what others complain about and create something to solve the problem.

Thoughts: Your thoughts are switching between life as you know it and what's truly available for you. You must learn how to effectively tap into your potential (your goals, dreams, and your purpose) and dramatically cut your learning curve.

The outer area of the PyramIT directly affects what's happening inside of the PyramIT.

On the left side of the PyramIT

Influence: The attack of our mind or our thoughts means we have become a valuable asset to the world. When we have thoughts that can change our life, we will be hit with all kinds of negative things because as we realize the POWER of possibility we move into a different dimension, a new level of consciousness that will change everything around us. So these attacks are to discourage us into believing it's not possible because of bad experiences in the past. It keeps us there, locked at the lowest level of our awareness. This level is full of doubt, fear and negative behaviors. The people around us may exhibit these same behaviors which will cause our consciousness to believe this has to be right, because everyone around us is thinking these same disempowering thoughts, so who am I to be different.

Working on your mind is important because what you think about, you bring about. You must hold the vision for what you want to accomplish.

Success leaves clues, you must find the people who are having success at whatever level you want to go to and follow what they do.

Choice: To take complete control of your life, you must make a decision to change the choices you have made in the past.

Accountability: Energy is power and in order to create a new life you must chose to give your energy to the things that have power to create change. This power begins with our words. There is nothing random about your life, it all has to do with how you perceive and react to every situation. Everything that happened in your life, the good and the bad, has graced you with a lesson.

Success: Every successful person has failed, you didn't know because we didn't see that part of the journey because they weren't famous when those things were happening and/or because they don't always talk about those trials. The most successful people aren't the people who never failed, they are the people who learned from their past failures, made adjustments, and tried again and again until they succeeded. Successful people are simply people who are persistent and tenacious when it comes to their IT. They probably heard "no" several times, but they chose to listen to what their inner power told them was possible.

Decisions: When you make a decision to change your "should" into a "can and will," your whole life changes. When you do whatever it takes to achieve your IT, and are willing to fail but continue anyway, that's when you know you are moving towards your PURPOSE.

On the right side of the PyramIT

Energy: Third law of physics, Newton's Law, is that for every action, there is an equal and opposite reaction. This energy extends to what we do, what we say, and, more importantly, who we are as we go into the world. For everything we put out in the world, there is an opposite reaction; whatever energy you put out will come back to you. Your purpose is designed to serve the energy of your soul.

Fear: Fear isn't real. It's only a product of our imaginations and causes us to believe things that may never exist. You aren't scared of the roller coaster, you're scared of the thoughts you have associated with the roller coaster, like what if it goes off the tracks, what if it stops and I get stuck on it, etc. Danger is real, but fear is a choice.

Action: In order to become all you were meant to be, you have to make a decision to leave where you are right now and trust in the pursuit of your IT. As you move away from your old energy, there will probably be a sense of loss because you are losing a part of who you used to be. Your main challenge will be to leave this old version of yourself to become the new version you desire. This version is following your IT. As you move toward this new energy, although it can be frustrating, you will find others who are moving up their PyramITs.

Belief: Once you begin to believe you are great and deserving of the success that will come to you, you will begin to develop a confidence that will be forced to succeed.

Focus: Focus is about staying disciplined in your approach by not allowing yourself to be distracted by the challenges that will come. If you remain steadfast in achieving the goals you have determined, you will achieve them.

The top of the PyramIT is the same as the bottom. The foundation that grounds the PyramIT, will also be at the height of the PyramIT, and must be sustained in order to continue living your IT.

Bottom of the PyramIT (RED)

Negative Behaviors: Many of these behaviors have been passed down by people who had them passed down from people who behaved negatively. Like you, they made a choice to emulate the people they were surrounded by.

Negative Thinking: The negative behaviors and thoughts you have been dealing with didn't just happen. Those things were sent to stop you from becoming all you were supposed to be. We have accepted some things in our life and have even adapted our way of living to these negative circumstances and created an acceptance to them. Now we view them as normal.

Faulty Belief System: Many of us have been programmed to believe certain things are possible or impossible. As a television or radio provides programming, this programming has taken place simply by what you have allowed to come into your mind, whether consciously or unconsciously. If you have been in an environment that believes you can't do something, then you have a tendency to believe what you have been told. This creates your belief system.

Bad Habits: Your habits determine how you live your life, and they are in direct proportion to your success. Habits aren't what you say you're going to do, they are what you actually do. Changing your bad habits to better habits requires you to push past what had previously been comfortable.

Doubt: You can't allow your fears and doubts to have more faith than what you believe is possible for your life. Your storm believes you have something inside of you that can change the world, which is why it came to stop you.

Helpless & Hopeless: We develop this sense of hopelessness based on the opinions of what others have believed is true for their life. We experience helplessness when we give up on any possibility of having hope. When we have been relying on others and they have let us down, and we forget we have a power inside of us to move moutains. After things become so overwhelming we rely less and less on this inside power to provide the very thing we yearn for.

Dysfunction: You have something in you that was designed for you, but storms and distractions have been distracting you from being all you were called to be. These distractions are taking away what is yours. It is our unwillingness to see things the way they are, and not worse than they are, to acknowledge the dysfunction we have been living in and not learning the tools needed to move to the next level.

Not Worthy: You can't change something you don't own. The unfortunate part of pain is that we allow it to keep us in a place of discontentment, because it tricks us into thinking we aren't worthy of having more. Often, our own pain causes us to inflict pain on ourselves and on the people around us. We may feel like we hate ourselves and we put that on those around us, blaming them for the situations we are in. This hate can cause harm to ourselves, and many times this pain is so deep rooted that the inward expression of this pain is shown through dysfunctional actions (i.e., drugs, alcohol, and/or rebellion).

Self Esteem: The fundamental key to success is having the belief and confidence to do what you want. You can say you want to be the most successful person in the world, but if you don't have confidence that you can do this, you will only go so far. You will be defined by the limits that you impose upon yourself.

Insecurity: The only time others can affect you is when you allow them to. When you feel confident about your purpose and are focused, disciplined, and committed, you realize it is only a distraction. You're not perfect and you don't need to be; staying persistent when it comes to your purpose and pushing through the negative thoughts and people will allow you to become stronger every day.

Not Smart Enough: Most of us, at some point in our lives, have felt we were not enough to achieve what we wanted.

Middle of the PyramIT (YELLOW)

Responsibility: You are responsible for the choices you make in your life. You are responsible for everything that happens and has happened in your life. I know this is a hard reality to swallow, and if you don't take responsibility for this you will never be healed from the event. Even though there is so much going on in the world, you must see the world as beautiful. Everything that has happened and is happening, is happening because it's supposed to. You only need to respond, knowing your place in this world is up to you. You and only you are responsible for your happiness.

Discipline: It's important to practice discipline daily; after all, practice makes (close to) perfect! Once you shift your understanding to the importance of your daily habits, your whole life will change. It's not the things you do once that determines your success, it's the things you consistently do. Self-discipline is a must for success. You learn to adhere to deadlines and meet the expectations not just for others, but for yourself as well. Discipline is not a feeling, it's an action. Be active!

Control: Control the words you speak and the words that you allow to come into your spirit. You have the power to control unwanted, disempowering words that try to invade your thoughts. Don't be arrogant, but be confident in the power you possess, have a steadfast understanding that you determine the results you want to see based on the actions you decide to take. It's not about having an arrogant, grandiose type of attitude, but walking with a confidence in knowing you've been educated and equipped with the knowledge to control your thoughts and actions.

New Beliefs: You control it all. Your success, purpose, and happiness is up to you. You have always been the captain of your life and able to determine the direction and course you set.

New Information: Information can never be taken away from you. You begin to understand the alignment of your purpose and how it has come to serve the world.

Middle of the PyramIT (BLACK)

Power: The confidence in knowing you have something inside you that created the world we currently live in. You have the power inside of you to be great, average, or below the level you deserve. It's up to your choices and attitudes to be as powerful as you want.

Top of the PyramIT (Green)

New Habits: The things that were once hard become easy once you do them. This is the key to success and purpose.

New Level of Consciousness: You have made mistakes and it's not the end of the world. We don't have to be perfect to experience our purpose, we only need to make progress toward it each day

Commitment: Commit yourself to becoming more aware, and determined to learn from your journey. Get excited about learning from your mistakes, and commit to creating the ongoing level of happiness you want. Our goals create our destiny! We must have enough compelling reasons to drive us forward to do whatever it takes to achieve our goals. What we're purposed to do is stronger than the results we receive. Who you become during the journey of achieving your goals is the real purpose.

Love: Be there in the moment for yourself and for others, don't worry about what they have done, but focus on what they are doing. Love yourself enough to understand that when a season ends in a relationship, it's time to begin being be there with and for people who will be there with and for you.

Confidence: You must be confident enough to know you can, regardless of what has happened in your past, not just because others have, although that's good and it helps. You can because you have something special inside of you. You have struggles and endured pain that would've caused an ordinary person to give up. You have a little extra that separates you from others, and when you combine your extra, with their ordinary, you then walk in the confidence of knowing that you are extraordinary.

The PyramIT of Purpose

Purpose/IT: Your IT is bigger than you are. You won't achieve your purpose because you hope for IT; you will only receive and experience your purpose by believing that it's possible and taking action to achieve it. In spite of the fluctuating economy, the rules for happiness have not changed. Anyone who has pursued and achieved their IT always find a way to make money.

Dr. D.F. Arnold

Day 20 — Human Needs

Serious problems arise when we choose destructive means to satisfy our needs. We must choose to establish new patterns of fulfilling our needs that will move us toward the life we truly deserve.

All human beings have the need for:

1. Control

We all want a sense we can avoid hurt and gain joy. Some people try to avoid hurt by trying to control everything around them. The paradox, though, is that when a person feels they are in total control, things can become predictable and make you bored. Therefore, while we want control, we simultaneously want a certain amount of surprise.

2. Change

Everyone craves change, a surprise, or a challenge to feel more alive and experience fulfillment. With too much control, we become complacent. Likewise, with too much change, we become fearful and concerned. We need a degree of comfort in our lives to appreciate the change. Some people choose to get variety, to feel a change in their MFAs, by doing drugs or alcohol. Others do it by watching movies. Others use stimulating conversation and opportunities to learn.

3. Purpose

We all have a need to discover our purpose, a sense of who we are on this earth. Again, we can try to meet this need through destructive means—making ourselves unique by, for example, manufacturing a belief we are better than everyone else. Some people become unique by developing extreme problems that set them apart from others. Some people believe they will find their purpose by earning more money, having more toys, going to school, and achieving more degrees.

4. Relationships

This includes feeling connected to yourself, as well as with others you can feel loved by and give love to. To meet this need, you can join a group or a club that has a positive purpose. Some individuals join a gang for negative purposes, but they still achieve the feeling of connection. As with all of your human needs, if you give that which you wish to receive, you tend to get it back from   others.

5. Growth

Growth equals life. On this planet, everything alive is either growing or dying. It all starts with awareness—you must become aware of why you are doing what you are doing now so you can find a new pattern for fulfillment!

YOUR ASSIGNMENT:

1. Write down two things you love doing—things you feel compelled to do and don't require any effort on your part. These are things you could do 24 hours a day, without being paid:

_____

_____

_____

_____

_____

_____

2. Describe a few things you hate doing, including things you should do, but it requires significant effort and you don't enjoy doint it:

_____

_____

_____

_____

_____

_____

3. Describe something you don't like to do, but you know it helps and is good for you and others, ultimately serving the greater good. Turn this up a notch by asking yourself, "What could I choose to believe about this that will make it feel like an opportunity, instead of a chore?" Write down your answers, then go out and take immediate action to make it happen.

_____

_____

_____

_____

_____

_____

Day 21 — What Will You Do?

Remember these key ideas:

1. Decide what it is that you truly want.

2. Develop an action plan, and find someone to be your mentor.

3. Immediately take action steps.

4. Remain flexible.

When you are feeling sad, mad, or indifferent, you must remember we are only happy in life if we are growing and contributing. What are you doing to contribute?

To live a life you truly deserve, I challenge you to do the following:

1. Master your MFAs.

2. Find reasons why it is necessary to control your emotions.

3. Find mentors who can help you deal with the challenges in your life.

4. Re-evaluate what you would like your life to look like. Be honest with yourself!

5. Be willing to help others; you will find great joy in this!

   a. Surround yourself with people who challenge you to be better and who you feel accountable to.

   b. Commit to be the best you possible. Demand greatness from yourself.

YOUR ASSIGNMENT:

1. Review the workbook section and complete any assignments or other work you have not yet finished.

2. Pick your top three goals and write a paragraph for each one, describing why you are committed to achieving it and what you have to lose by not achieving it.

3. Develop a plan for achieving these three goals, including what you can do immediately toward accomplishing each.

Congratulations on the new momentum you have created in your life!

The PyramIT of Purpose

Please consider allowing me the privilege of coaching you personally. By reading the materials in the back of this book, you will discover if you would like to participate in our online event. At the very least, I would greatly appreciate it if you would stay in touch by writing to me to share what this program has done for you.

I can promise that if you allow me to work with you personally, I will assist you in taking whatever changes you made over the past 21 days to an even greater level for more success and fulfillment than you have imagined.

Dr. D.F. Arnold

Conclusion

I hope you have enjoyed reading The PyramIT of Purpose, and have benifited from the exercises. The assignments were designed to help you get a handle on what has distracted from your true calling, and to help start you on the process of discovering your PURPOSE.

I want to encourage you to keep growing. Review your PyramIT daily, and read this book periodically to measure how you're developing. Put yourself on a regular program where you consistently read books, listen to thought leaders, watch inspirational videos and attend conferences that stretch you. If you're looking for resources to help you with that process, contact my organization.

We'll be glad to send you a catalog and current conference schedule. I also want to encourage you to find other leaders who will mentor you in person or through books and videos. The only way to stay in the green on your PyramIT, is to stay Focused on the decision you made to follow your PURPOSE.

Dr. D.F. Arnold

PyramIT of PURPOSE

Are you ready to discover your Purpose? **The PyramIT of Purpose** gives you the COMPLETE, PROVEN SYSTEM for using the potential you have locked inside of you to achieve financial, emotional, physical and spiritual prosperity. The *PyramIT of Purpose System* will open your eyes to the deep reservoirs of talent and ability that lie deep inside you. The *PyramIT of Purpose System* contains the complete plan for discovering your purpose and unlocking the untapped potential in every aspect of your life.

Here's just some of what you will learn in this life-changing program:

- How to successfully balance the emotional, intellectual, and physical parts of your being

- What's causing you to receive your current results— and how to change any result your aren't hapy with.

- How to use the natural laws of the universe for your maximum benefit

- The most effective way to change any habit

- The little known secrets of how your mind really works – and how to use "IT" to get the most out of your mental processes

- The Formula for Financial Freedom

Dr. D.F. Arnold has been the foremost authority in the personal and professional development field for more than 15 years. He has dedicated his adult life to helping a world of individuals realize and act on the greatness they already possess within themselves. His transformational talks and seminars have made him one of the elite teachers in personal development. **Dr. D.F. Arnold** is a genius businessman and expert committed to improving the conscious awareness of the entire world, one individual at a time.

What you will receive:

Includes the complete 2-hour in person workshop or one 50-minute DVD –for your learning pleasure; best-selling book, *The PyramIT of Purpose* along with your Personal Action Planner.

What people are saying about the PyramIT of Purpose Program

I have read plenty self-help books. Some of the most noteworthy are Napoleon's Hill's 'Think and Grow Rich' and Anthony Robbin's 'Awaken the Giant Within'. There are, in fact, only a few books out there that are of the top-quality content. This is because most of them are simply made up of recycled concepts and ideas and the worst part is that they are pretty theoretical. However, I have to say that I was stumped by the content of the PyramIT of Purpose – in a positive light.

The PyramIT of Purpose not only contains comprehensive system on how to discover your purpose, but also concrete action plans for the reader to follow. The book also contains a workbook for the reader to write down their goals and steps that they plan to take. I personally believe that this is a fundamental step in goal-setting.

Even though most books on self-improvement and motivation are merely the same concepts used over and over again, I have to say that this book serves more than just a repackaged content from some other self-help books. It is an elaboration which explains in detail what those success concepts are to discover your purpose and the practical steps required.

Besides that, the ideas in the book are presented in a clear simple-to-understand language. That is important for readers to digest the information in the book. This is because many self-help books out there are written in a complicated language which not many readers can grasp easily

Another factor which I like about the PyramIT of Purpose is that it combines some practical applications. This is something which I find unique about the book unlike some other self-help books which simply mentions theories that are easier said than done.

As a conclusion, I strongly believe that a lot of people can benefit from the book and the workshop. Its content, presented in a clear and concise manner, is very comprehensive and straight to the point.

It is jam-packed with practical steps which you can take and follow.

For information...Call 855-9LIVEIT(954-8348) or 616-482-9291 www.dfarnold.com

CPSIA information can be obtained
at www.ICGtesting.com
Printed in the USA
FSHW021204181218